Modern Critical Interpretations

Homer's
The Odyssey

Modern Critical Interpretations

These and other titles in preparation

Homer's
The Odyssey

Edited and with an introduction by
Harold Bloom
Sterling Professor of the Humanities
Yale University

Chelsea House Publishers
NEW YORK ◊ PHILADELPHIA

Printed and bound in the United States of America

10 9 8 7 6 5 4

∞ The paper used in this publication meets the minimum
requirements of the American National Standard for Permanence
of Paper for Printed Library Materials, Z39.48–1984.

Library of Congress Cataloging-in-Publication Data
Homer's the Odyssey.
   (Modern critical interpretations)
   Bibliography: p.
   Includes index.
   Summary: A collection of seven critical essays on Homer's
epic poem, arranged chronologically in order of their original
publication.
   1. Homer. Odyssey.   2. Odysseus (Greek mythology) in
literature.   [1. Homer. Odyssey.   2. Odysseus (Greek
mythology) in literature.   3. Classical literature—History and
criticism]   I. Bloom, Harold.   II. Series.
PA4167.H66 1988   833'.01   87–13849
ISBN 1–55546–043–7

Contents

Editor's Note

This book gathers together a representative selection of the best modern critical interpretations of Homer's *Odyssey.* The critical essays are reprinted here in the chronological order of their original publication. I am grateful to Ingrid Holmberg for her assistance in editing this volume.

My introduction briefly considers the salient differences between the *Iliad* and the *Odyssey,* centering upon the contrasts between Achilles and Odysseus. H. D. F. Kitto begins the chronological sequence of criticism with an overview of the epic that charts a common aesthetic element it shares with the Athenian tragedies: the exclusion of surprise.

The epic function of the homecomings of the Achaean heroes is analyzed by Agathe Thornton, after which C. M. Bowra surveys the nature of the *Odyssey* with particular reference to its contrasts with the *Iliad.*

Norman Austin presents a vision of the *Odyssey* as a poem whose language celebrates the civilized values of domestic harmony, or *homophrosyne,* demonstrating how much of the epic's action is actually conversation. In an allied but very different essay, Helene P. Foley describes the relation between sex roles and rhetoric in the poem.

Interpreting the name of Odysseus and the significance of his helmet, Jenny Strauss Clay aids us in comprehending the complex nature of the elusive hero, man of many wiles. In this book's final essay, Charles Segal considers the ironies of heroic glory, or *kleos,* in the *Odyssey* and the relationship of that concept to *dolos,* or skill in trickery, and *aidos,* or shame.

Introduction

The *Odyssey,* though a clear sequel to the *Iliad,* is an immensely different poem in the experience of all readers. If one author wrote both, then the change from the *Iliad* to the *Odyssey* is as great as the difference between *War and Peace* and *Anna Karenina,* or between *Paradise Lost* and *Paradise Regained.* Such comparisons suggest a darkening of vision in Homer, as in Tolstoy or Milton, but of course the movement from *Iliad* to *Odyssey* is from tragic to comic, from epic to romance, from the rage of Achilles against mortality to the prudence of Odysseus in recovering wife, son, father, home, and kingdom. The *Iliad,* in fierce agon with the Bible, has set our standards for sublimity, but the *Odyssey* has been the more fecund work, particularly in modern literature. Joyce did not write a novel called *Achilles,* nor did Pound and Stevens devote poems to the hero of the *Iliad.* Like Dante and Tennyson before them, they became obsessed with Ulysses, whose quest for home contrasts oddly with the role of anti-Aeneas assigned to him by Dante and, more uneasily, by Tennyson.

A permanent mystery of the contrast between *Iliad* and *Odyssey* is that the *Iliad* seems much farther away from us, though it has less of the fantastic or the fabulous than the *Odyssey.* Achilles is a remote Sublime, whereas Odysseus is the complete man of Joyce's vision, coping with the everyday. Realistic description of marvels is the romance formula of the *Odyssey* and seems very different from the tragic world in which Achilles and Hector strive to be the best. A literary critic who is not a classicist, and with indifferent Greek, nevertheless takes away from both epics an overwhelming sense of the unity of very separate designs in the immense consciousness of a comprehensive poet coming very late in a tradition. Samuel Johnson, my critical hero, darkly judged every Western poet coming after Homer to be belated. It is a productive irony that Johnson seems

1

to me correct as to the *Iliad,* but that the *Odyssey* overwhelmingly strikes me as the epic of belatedness, the song of things-in-their-farewell.

We cannot envision Achilles existing in the day-to-day world of the *Odyssey,* which cannot accommodate so single-minded a hero. You go west, to the Islands of the Dead, to find the great Achilles or the frustrated spirit of Ajax, doomed always to be the second best. The Odysseus of Homer, superbly unlike the anti-Aeneas of Dante and Tennyson, is the true prototype of Aeneas, but Virgil's priggish moralist is an involuntary travesty of the hero of the *Odyssey.* Poor Aeneas actually must carry the emperor Augustus on his back, while Odysseus is free of ideology, unless the desire to reclaim what was once your own is to be considered a politics of the spirit.

Achilles, as critics note, is somewhat childlike, but Odysseus has had to put away childish things and lives in a world where you can freeze to death, as well as be devoured by one-eyed monsters. Self-control, a virtue alien to Achilles, is hardly a poetic quality as such and in Odysseus seems unallied to any system of morality. Americans justly find in Homer's later hero the first pragmatist, unimpressed by differences that do not make a difference. Existence, for the necessarily cunning Odysseus, is a vast obstacle course that has kept you away from home for a full decade and that will exercise you for a second decade as you voyage back. When you get there, your largest ordeal begins, since a slaughter in your own home, even with yourself as shrewd slaughterer, is an altogether more daunting prospect than even the most ferocious battling upon the windy plain of Troy.

Joyce's Ulysses, the humane though masochistic Poldy, is the most amiable personage in all literature, despite the absurd moralizings against him of Modernist critics. Homer's Odysseus is a very dangerous figure, whom we admire and respect but do not love. He is a great survivor, the one man who will stay afloat when all his shipmates drown. You would not want to be in one boat with him then, but there is no one you would rather read or hear about, because survival is the best of all stories. Stories exist to defer death, and Odysseus is a grand evader of mortality, unlike the tragic Achilles, who rages against being only half a god, yet who is pragmatically doom-eager. The agon of Achilles, the best of the Achaeans, is thus of a different order than the sensible ecstasy of Odysseus, who fights only when he must and always for sharply delineated ends. The desire for the foremost place recedes, and the will to live another day takes on its own aura of heroism.

The enmity of Poseidon is so great a burden for an island-king who needs to voyage back that Odysseus has only the two choices: heroic endurance or death, unless he wishes to forget household and hearth and yield to one of the manifold temptations that are made available to him. He is not exactly a yielder, and consequently he has provided a model for every striver since. The model, as Dante and even Tennyson show, is a dangerous one, since it encourages the development of the ability to deceive others. But if the cosmos of water and wind is against you and you cannot stay on the mainland, then you must choose the remaining element and speak out of the fire, as Dante's Ulysses does. Fire, which in the *Iliad* is associated with death in battle, becomes in the *Odyssey* a trope for survival, the light not of flashing arms and armor but of the hearth where Penelope holds court, delaying the suitors while waiting for the pragmatic or belated hero to return to her, never forgetting him that kept coming so close:

> Now from his breast into his eyes the ache
> of longing mounted, and he wept at last,
> his dear wife, clear and faithful, in his arms,
> longed for as the sunwarmed earth is longed for by a swimmer
> spent in rough water where his ship went down
> under Poseidon's blows, gale winds and tons of sea.
> Few men can keep alive through a big surf
> to crawl, clotted with brine, on kindly beaches
> in joy, in joy, knowing the abyss behind:
> and so she too rejoiced, her gaze upon her husband,
> her white arms round him pressed as though forever.
>   (Translated by Robert Fitzgerald)

The *Odyssey:*
The Exclusion of Surprise

H. D. F. Kitto

It would be reasonable to go straight from Aeschylus to Sophocles, but some writers are not entirely reasonable. If first we go backwards, to Homer and the *Odyssey,* we shall, for one thing, have a change of scenery, which may be some relief, and for another thing we shall see that poiesis is by no means a matter of dramatic composition only—a point that was very clear to my distinguished predecessor in this field, the Stagirite.

There are two Homeric questions. There is the one first asked by Lachmann and eagerly debated ever since: one Homer, or two, or a multitude? The other is: What are the poems about? How did Homer think? We can consider the poems either as historic monuments (which they are), or as poems (which they are). I admit that the two questions are not entirely separable. It is indeed possible to examine some purely archae-ological, philological, or historical aspects of the poems without consid-ering their poetic qualities at all, but, ideally, one cannot do the converse. If this chapter takes very little notice of the more famous Homeric ques-tion, the reason is that it is concerned with the *Odyssey,* as a poem, from a particular point of view: we shall be using it as a means of testing Aristotle's assertion that structure, "the disposition of the material," is all-important. We will test it by performing a kind of experiment. I choose the *Odyssey* rather than the *Iliad* because its structure is more taut, and it is more taut because the *Iliad*—notably in the Catalogue of the Ships—incorporates much more quasi-historical material. If the same poet wrote both poems, on which question I need express no opinion

From *Poiesis: Structure and Thought.* © 1966 by the Regents of the University of Cal-ifornia. University of California Press, 1966.

here, he was much more conscious in the *Iliad* of having a function additional to that of being a profoundly tragic epic poet.

For the purposes of this chapter I shall assume what is in any case obvious, that some major poet gave to the *Odyssey* what is substantially its present shape. Book 6 may be a later addition; I can afford to express no opinion because the present argument would not be affected; still less would minor interpolations affect it. Other suspected passages will be considered as they turn up.

It is traditional to say that the structure of the poem is one of the surest signs of the poet's genius. The raw material of which it is composed is abundant and diverse, far flung both in time and space, yet it is organised by Homer into a plot of the utmost clarity and simplicity, so that the action occupies only thirty-seven days. Is this not a masterstroke? Certainly—but let us not suppose that when we say this we are saying anything of great importance. The plot is an example of poiesis on the grand scale, and poiesis has to do with more than literary skill: it has something to do with mind and thought. To illustrate the point I have composed and here present the plot of a new *Odyssey*. It uses the same material as Homer's (or as nearly as makes no difference), but disposes it in an entirely different way. The reader is asked to imagine my plot to be realised in a poem by a poet not inferior to Homer: by a poet, I mean, with all of Homer's humanity, vividness, power, with all of Homer's delight in everything that he sees or imagines in the world about him, whether wicked pirates, faithful servants, enterprising traders, or wine-dark seas in fair weather or tempest, or gentlefolk enjoying their games, or a beggar scrounging at a rich man's gate; whether impossible marvels like Circe, the horrible Laestrygonians, the lawless Cyclops, or nearly possible ones like Nausicaa and her god-fearing relatives. If the reader will do this, then two questions will follow. The first: if the great Homer had used my plot, should we not now be saying about it exactly what we say about his, that it shows literary genius? The second: what happens now to the innocent idea that the Greek dramatists merely dramatised saga, since we shall have here precisely the same saga-material set forth in utterly different ways, and meaning (as we shall see) utterly different things in consequence?

For yet another reason I have undertaken this enterprise. By different men at different times grave faults have been found in the *Odyssey* and variously explained: from my alternative poem it will become clear, I hope, that the faults should be imputed not to Homer but to the critics, for they have assumed without question that Homer was trying to do

one thing, and in some respects doing it not very well (unless an interpolator can be blamed), when in fact he was trying to do something
rather different, something that lay outside their personal experience of
literature; and that instead of trying to enlarge their own experience by
studying Homer's poiesis and drawing the obvious inferences from it,
they found it more natural, and certainly easier, to blame the poet.

Let us first review some of these criticisms, beginning, as is right
and proper, with that excellent early-modern critic Longinus—for Longinus, after all, was separated from Homer by about a thousand years,
and in social structure and habits of thought the Roman Empire was as
alien from the Homeric age as our own is. In his impressive comparison
of the *Odyssey* with the *Iliad* Longinus writes like this:

> The *Odyssey* shows that when a great genius is in decline, a
> special mark of old age is the love of telling stories. The *Od-
> yssey* is Homer's later poem, an epilogue to the *Iliad.* The *Iliad,*
> written when Homer's inspiration was at its height, is full of
> action and conflict; the *Odyssey* for the most part consists of
> narrative, the characteristic of old age. It is the sunset of Ho-
> mer: the grandeur remains, but not the intensity. You seem to
> see the ebb and flow of greatness, a fancy that roams through
> the fabulous and the incredible; it is as if the Ocean were
> withdrawing into itself, leaving its bed here and there high
> and dry. I have not forgotten the tempests of the *Odyssey,* the
> story of the Cyclops, and the like; if I speak of old age, it is
> nevertheless the old age of Homer. Yet throughout the poem
> as a whole, the fabulous prevails over the real. Genius, when
> it has passed its prime, can sink into absurdity—for example,
> the incident of the wine-skin, of a hero on a wreck for ten
> days without food, of the incredible slaying of the Suitors.
> Another sign of old age is fondness for the delineation of man-
> ners; for such are the details that Homer gives, with an eye
> for description, of life in the house of Odysseus; they form,
> as it were, a Comedy of Manners (κωμῳδία ἠθολογουμένη).

Longinus, then, found that the *Odyssey* lacks the grandeur and intensity of the *Iliad*—and few will quarrel with him for that—but his
criticism fails; it illuminates Longinus, but not Homer. It fails because he
comes to the poem with a specific demand, namely that it should display
epic sublimity, and when he finds that it does not do this, instead of
asking whether it meets different demands he finds a less laborious ex-

planation: Homer, when he came to write the *Odyssey,* was quite an old gentleman, past his best, a bit garrulous, φιλόμυθος, interested now in quiet things like the delineation of character and manners. It is of course an impressive passage, but the criticism is of that unconstructive kind that is content with negatives: "Aeschylus was not so clever as Sophocles in constructing plots"; "Thucydides had no idea of the importance of economic affairs"; "the slaying of the Suitors is incredible."

From this springboard I jump to a modern critic of the poem—a scientist, once a colleague of my own, therefore an intelligent and civilized man. He read the *Odyssey,* in E. V. Rieu's translation, and told me how much he had enjoyed it: so vivid and entrancing a story. But he, like Longinus, boggled at the slaying of the Suitors, though not for the same reason. What was merely incredible—the wine-skin and suchlike, he, being a scientist, could take in his stride; what worried him was the gods, especially Athena, popping up from time to time to make things easier for Odysseus, particularly in the fight with the Suitors, stealing the hero's thunder, "making him look half a fool."

This critic, like Longinus, was looking at the poem, naturally, from his own point of view, and that was something like this: "In the poem I find things familiar to me. There is a hero in distress. He has one ambition, to get home. He meets difficulties of all kinds, but being bold, resourceful, and courageous he surmounts them. Some of the incidents are marvellous, but *that* does not upset me. He does get back home, is confronted with a final test, passes it triumphantly, and all is well. It is that familiar thing, an adventure story, and it is supremely well told. Incidents like those of Circe or the Cyclops confirm my diagnosis. But in a tale of this kind, gods are a nuisance—at least, gods who pull the strings for the hero at a crisis."

And what do we say in reply? Useless to talk to a scientist about "the epic tradition of divine machinery." He would be quick to point out that this only says again, in different words, that Homer used gods even when they are a nuisance to his story; and he might well ask if the Greeks were such that the greatest of their poets lacked the courage or the originality to throw overboard a tradition when it was cramping and cumbrous.

Then there is Telemachus's journey to Sparta. It is an attractive episode, and, as Aristotle wisely said, the epic form is hospitable to such—but does it *do* anything for us, and for the poem, other than decorate it, at rather undue length? Because when at last Telemachus does return, the little news that he has been able to pick up is already out of date, since Homer contrives that Odysseus should get home first. Naturally, it has been suggested that this part of the *Odyssey* was originally a separate lay, having Telemachus for its hero. Very well; but whose idea was it to bring it into the *Odyssey*? It may indeed be a law of nature that an interpolator is a fool as well as a nuisance, but if the interpolation is so obviously useless, why ever did it remain in the poem? In fact, as Delabecque has shown, in his *Télémaque et la structure de l'Odyssée,* the episode is so carefully worked into the main fabric, with so many deft links, that if Homer did not himself compose it (which he may well have done), he at least adopted it, quite deliberately, and therefore with some idea in mind. What was it?

One part of the episode is even more challenging, namely the long description in book 2 of the Assembly held in Ithaca, for it accomplishes practically nothing. Telemachus calls the meeting, makes a protest against the Suitors, and receives very little support; then he demands a ship, gets consent of a kind—and immediately acquires a ship by other means: through the agency of Athena. What is the point of it all? It is easy to make it sound inept; what is not so easy is to make such a degree of ineptitude sound plausible, even by invoking an interpolator.

One might also ask about the whole theme of the Suitors if it is not a little bourgeois. That young gallants should riot in the house of an absent man, waste his substance, and persecute his wife (or widow) is deplorable conduct indeed, but is it of epic dignity, worthy of being set alongside the tragic theme of Achilles' wrath? Longinus evidently thought not; to him it was only Comedy of Manners.

Then, naturally, there is the ending of the poem. (I say "naturally" because the Greeks were notoriously bad at endings: the *Iliad, Odyssey, Antigone, Ajax, Trachiniae, Medea:* an impressive list.) There is some consensus of opinion that Homer ended his poem at book 23, line 296, where Odysseus and Penelope are reunited and Athena prolongs the night for their comfort and joy. The poem we have goes past this point to what Myres called "a poor, drivelling, misbegotten end": the friends of the slain Suitors (as Myres put it) prepare to take vengeance on Odysseus and his party; these in turn arm themselves with zest, so that old Laertes cries out in delight: "Dear gods! What a day is this to warm my heart! My son and grandson are competing in valour." But Athena intervenes with a great cry to make them all drop their weapons and conclude a peace—and Myres, himself the gallant commander of a gunboat in the First World War, is bitterly disappointed, and refuses to debit an ending like this to Homer.

Here, then, are some features of the poem which, from time to time, have been found weak, puzzling, or spurious. We will put them into cold storage for a short time while we contemplate Homer's σύσ-τασις τῶν πϱαγμάτων; then we will take them out for a second look.

The immense variety and amplitude of Homer's raw material need not be expounded in detail. There are, to begin with, the many and various echoes of the Trojan War: the Wooden Horse; the calamitous return of Agamemnon; Menelaus's wanderings, and his return, with Helen; Helen herself, living in royal splendour at Sparta; Nestor, Achilles, Ajax, and other heroes among the shades (if book 11 is genuine). Then there are the many fabulous marvels with which the imagination of the Greeks and others had filled the unknown reaches of the sea—some of them immemorial folktales. There are the many vivid sketches taken from contemporary life—pirates, beggars, and the rest. It is God's plenty, and all is set down with the greatest possible enthusiasm and solidity. If in other respects the poem were a complete mess, with all this material loosely stuffed into sacks, it would still give inexhaustible pleasure.

But upon all this profusion Homer has imposed a form which is clarity itself. The masterstroke, as Horace pointed out, was the decision to begin in medias res—in fact, near the end, with Odysseus, already for seven years a prisoner, now on the point of being set free. This, the starting point, is made clear with great brevity; very cunningly Homer keeps back the story of Odysseus's wanderings, those past and those to come, so that we may have them in unbroken sequence. For the tale of the past wanderings he contrives the perfect setting: it is told by the suffering hero himself, and to an audience that has dined well, has been enormously impressed by the stranger's prowess at games, and is prepared to listen, if need be, all night. This half of the material is enfolded within the other half—all that concerns Ithaca and Telemachus: after his brief proem, Homer begins where he is going to end, in Ithaca. The poem is made to circle round itself, like a snake; or, since there are those who do not much care for snakes, let us say rather that Homer designed his poem in what musicians call ternary form, A—B—A: Ithaca, with the son seeking news of his father—the whole story of Odysseus's wanderings—Ithaca, and the triumph of father and son. (Current attempts to explain Homer's form as a reflection of the sculptured pediment, or of geometric art, exercise the fancy rather than nourish the understanding. A poem exists in time, the visual arts in space. I cannot see what point there can be in saying that a town hall is in the form of a sonnet, or a limerick in the form of a petrol station. I know that Erik Satie composed

Trois Morceaux en forme d'une poire, but that was intended to be amusing. What there is in common between the sense of form of Homer and of his contemporary painters and designers must be sought at a deeper level than this.)

We say that one sign of Homer's literary skill is that on such varied material he was able to impose a form so simple—but we need to be careful. Both Plato and Aristotle, as it happens, compare a work of art to a ζῷον, a living creature, complete and purposeful in every detail. It may be that their metaphor commends itself; but our talk of "imposing" a form suggests the carpenter rather than the creator. I think that it could be argued (though I would not care to undertake it) that this ternary form of Homer's already implies something, vague though it may be, about his mind and habit of thought; I do not believe that he selected this out of several possible forms merely by the exercise of literary judgment. The form itself implies too much. Perhaps the point will be made clear from my alternative *Odyssey,* which I now submit to the reader's admiration.

My poem begins at Troy. The war has just ended. Odysseus and his men load rich booty into their little fleet, and they set sail, after so many years, for Ithaca. Odysseus, in one mood, rejoices at the prospect of seeing wife and son again; in another, he wonders anxiously if he still has a wife and son. Yet they are quite willing to do a little piracy on the way, so that (as in Homer's narrative) they raid the Cicones: they gain some plunder, though some of the men are lost; the others sail on, glad at heart at their escape but lamenting the loss of their dear companions. The other incidents happen one by one, as in Homer, caused whether by the gods or by the folly of Odysseus's men. So, little by little, the glory slips away, the bright hopes fade; what was at first eager expectation slowly turns to despair. This downward movement continues implacably until Odysseus alone is left, the sole survivor of the fleet, cast ashore on Calypso's island.

Here is the nadir of his fortunes. He is a prisoner, aching to get home—and it is a capital point that neither Odysseus nor the reader knows if he still has a wife and home to return to. But at last the tide turns; the gods resolve that Calypso must let him go to take his chance. Now the long downward movement is answered by a vigorous upward movement. Odysseus battles hard, but—alas!—again he is shipwrecked. Will he again fall victim to a beautiful but baleful goddess—or even worse? No! This island is inhabited by the kind and god-fearing Phaeacians. They cannot indeed tell Odysseus—or us—anything about Ithaca,

Penelope, and Telemachus, but at least they know where Ithaca is. So, after proper entertainment, they send him there, and he is home at last.

It is at this point that the constructive skill of the present poet becomes most evident. We have climbed back, roughly speaking, to the emotional level on which the poem began: Odysseus had left Troy for Ithaca; now he is in Ithaca. Being wily, as well as anxious, and remembering the trusty swineherd, he thinks it prudent to pay him a visit before going near the city. Eumaeus is still there, still trusty.—That is good!—Odysseus learns from him that Penelope and Telemachus are both alive and well.—That is very good!—But now there comes a double check. The first is the fact that Odysseus's house and property are at the mercy of a wild gang of Suitors, and that Penelope, at last, being almost persuaded that Odysseus must be dead, is on the point of choosing another husband. What is worse, Laertes has withdrawn in despair, and nobody in Ithaca shows any disposition to control the violence of these men. When these untoward facts have been properly exploited by the poet, Eumaeus gives the rest of his grave news. It is barely a month since Telemachus—so gallant a young man, so like his father—left Ithaca for Pylos, Sparta, goodness knows where, in search of news about his father; and not only that: the Suitors have laid an ambush for him, to murder him on his way home—if indeed he does find the homeward path from that treacherous sea that Odysseus himself knows so well. It is a bitterly ironical turn of circumstance that as soon as the wandering hero returns in safety, it becomes a question whether his son can ever return.

When our second Homer has had the time to make the most of this unlucky situation, he may bring back Telemachus in safety—by all means with the help of Athena, provided that Athena has not spoiled the story by declaring in advance that this is what she is going to do. Father and son are now reunited, and at last the dramatic rhythm of the whole poem gathers all its force for a final upward thrust that will carry us, with barely a check, to the triumphant conclusion. The two men will gather around them a few faithful retainers; by cunning and courage they will give the Suitors what they deserve—though of course not until we have been shown how fully they deserve it—and at last the long-tried husband and wife are at peace in their own home. Here the poem ends.

Certainly I am no impartial judge, but I fail to see how this plot is intrinsically inferior to Homer's. Obviously it lacks some of the specific virtues of Homer's; for one thing, the action is not so concise. On the other hand, it has countervailing virtues: its control of dramatic rhythm strikes me as being particularly fine, especially in the double check, which—just at the right moment—infuses new and vigorous life into the plot. But if this is true, then we have not said the last word, but only the first, when we have said that Homer's ordering of the material shows literary genius. Of course it does, but something more than craftsmanship is involved in poiesis; there is more than one way of being an excellent craftsman.

As for my plot, the reader may well feel like echoing what Bentley said to Pope: "A very pretty poem, Mr Kitto, but it is not Homer." Of course we are postulating in our own poet a full command of surge and thunder, but that will not be enough; my poem will never be Homeric. What is more interesting is that my plot, from the bottom upwards, is entirely un-Hellenic; conceivably Hellenistic, but certainly not Hellenic. If this is true, we must ask why.

Comparing my plot with Homer's, we see at once that mine has rejected Homer's ternary form in favour of one which swings along with vigour, up or down, but always forwards. This difference, evidently, is connected with the major difference, which is emotional and mental: my poem relies throughout on suspense and surprise; Homer's does not, except in a subordinate way. When my poem begins, we lean back comfortably in our seats to hear what is going to happen to the hero. It may be almost anything, and I say *almost* anything because there is one thing that must not happen to him, namely ultimate disaster. With increasing apprehension we shall follow him on his downward path; with increasing hope on his upward path. Like him, we shall be suddenly cast down when we discover, after the excitement of his arrival in Ithaca, how desperate the situation there is; we shall ask ourselves anxiously if Odysseus has survived all these perils only for his son to be overwhelmed by worse. Then, relieved on this score, with growing excitement we shall follow their daring adventures to the final triumph. Yet all the time, deep down, we shall have felt the assurance, though sometimes a little tremulously, that surely all will come right in the end. Why? Because it always does, in romantic adventure stories—and that is precisely what I have made, out of Homer's own material: the plot of a romance, with the typical shape and movement of a romance. The reason why a disastrous ending is impossible is that it would blow this delightful world to pieces.

My plot depends on suspense, on keeping the listener in ignorance. Homer will have nothing to do with this; he is as careful to forestall surprise as I have been to create it. Naturally, in Homer's plot also, Odysseus never knows what is going to happen next, nor for that matter do we, the readers; but *we* do know what is going to happen last, because

Homer tells us at the beginning of book 1, and again at the beginning of book 5; and throughout the poem, but especially in the second half, the destruction of the Suitors is foreshadowed repeatedly. My poem carefully keeps back from the reader what has been happening all these years in Ithaca; it is with this that Homer begins. By way of proem he invents the scene on Olympus, with the philosophic speech from Zeus: "Men are born to trouble in any case, but they make things far worse for themselves by their own wickedness—and then blame us gods. Take Aegisthus for instance." "Then what about Odysseus?" says Athena, with the result that she is given permission to see that he gets home. "We will deliberate," says Zeus, "how it shall be done." Therefore the return of Odysseus is no tremulous hope; it is a certainty.

From Olympus we go in Athena's company straight to Ithaca and spend some long time there, enough to see with our own eyes what is going on. Odysseus of course knows nothing, but *we* do; it is not being kept back from us, as in my poem.

After going to Pylos and Sparta with Athena and Telemachus and much enjoying the trip, for Homer is a lively poet, we return to Olympus, at the beginning of book 5. It is an old complaint, that the second Council of Gods is only a duplication of the first. In fact, it is not. At the first council, the subject to which Zeus was addressing his unfathomable mind was Aegisthus; the case of Odysseus was raised from the floor of the house by Athena, and only an interim decision was taken; a second meeting, to deal more particularly with Odysseus, was implied, and here it is. Besides, this time Athena is more outspoken, and this time she has more to be outspoken about. At the first council the misdeeds of the Suitors were mentioned only incidentally (1.91f.); this time, when we have seen something of it for ourselves, Athena says more: that no one in Ithaca is giving a single thought to the excellent king who once ruled them like a wise and kind father; and, what is worse, the Suitors are now actually plotting to murder his son. "What king need practise kindness, generosity, justice, if tyranny and lawlessness go unpunished?"

A second opportunity for dramatic surprise has been thrown away. It was a powerful turn in my plot that Odysseus reaches Ithaca only to learn that Telemachus has just left it and is in peril of being murdered on his way home. Homer will have none of this: he makes Zeus instruct Athena to take care of Telemachus; therefore we know that he will be safe. My plot revels in the appeal to certain emotions—anxiety, in this case—in which Homer has little interest. Then (ll. 29ff.) Zeus is made to announce his plan for Odysseus: he shall be set free, shall make a boat, reach Scheria, and be conveyed to Ithaca—a plan which is much better placed here than it would have been at the beginning of book 1. The second council is no interpolation; one sometimes wonders if some of the most disruptive of Homer's critics have themselves ever read a book.

Surprise then, major surprise, is in general excluded: we already know roughly what is going to happen to Odysseus. So too is it excluded in respect of the Battle in the Hall: there is no lack of excitement in the details, but since we have been told explicitly that Athena and Zeus are helping Odysseus, the result of the fight is certain.

But is there not something familiar in this forestalling of surprise? Indeed there is: it is normal in the Greek tragic poets. Not only do they, like most tragic poets, and like Homer, use myths which in general outline were already known; they also regularly foreshadow the important event of the play. We may be taken aback by the manner or the extent of the disaster, but not by the disaster itself. In the *Agamemnon,* who is surprised by the murder of the king—who, I mean, other than the king himself? The chorus is surprised that he should be killed now, and by his wife, but retribution of some kind they distinctly feared; and as for the audience, the killing of Agamemnon, Cassandra, Clytemnestra, Aegisthus, is carefully prepared. So too is the liberation of Prometheus, the self-blinding of Oedipus, the defeat of the Persians, the downfall of Creon (in the *Antigone*), the destruction of Phaedra and Hippolytus, of the children in the *Medea.*

What are we to say about this? That the Athenians, being timid people, disliked surprises; or, being dull people, could not follow a play unless they were told the plot in advance? For at least two reasons this kind of thing will not do. One is that among the extant plays there are some that rely on surprise from beginning to end: the *Iphigeneia in Tauris* for example, the *Ion,* and *Helen. * Agathon's *Antheus* was probably of this type, since here, as Aristotle tells us, the dramatist took the trouble to invent both the plot and the characters. In the *Ion* indeed, in order to accentuate the surprise, Euripides wrote a prologue in which Hermes foreshadows a conclusion at which the play fails to arrive, evidently to increase the piquancy. The second of the two reasons is that Shakespeare too . . . foreshadows in much the same way, and that both Shakespeare and the Athenian dramatists foreshadow when they are composing tragedy and avoid it when writing a less profound kind of drama.

But does this help us at all, seeing that the *Odyssey,* for all its forestalling of surprise, is not a tragedy? It may help a lot, if we will look a little further.

The reason why the tragic poets, Greek or English, discount surprise is that they are concerned with that serious aspect of human existence in which law prevails, in which offence will incur disaster, in which the very nature of things will have the last word. Thus, in the matter of the Persian War, to Aeschylus the Athenian citizen the outcome was no doubt astonishing, but to Aeschylus the tragic poet it was natural, and to indicate that it was natural he involves gods in the action (which accordingly some of us interpret to mean that it was unnatural or supernatural). This is what Homer does too; and he was thoughtful enough to assist my present argument by being quite explicit about it, in the two Councils of the Gods. In rearranging Homer's material I saw an opportunity of constructing a romantic story, one which should obey the principle implicit in plays like the *Iphigeneia:* keep the cat in the bag as long as possible; then, when the audience is quite sure that the bag is empty, produce another cat. Much has been said about the romantic colouring of the *Odyssey:* there is no need whatever to object, so long as we are clear that it is a matter of colouring only, not of structure and substance. Homer, in constructing his plot, worked from what we must surprisingly call a religious point of view. It is true that his "religion" is neither Platonic nor strict Presbyterian (for these do have something in common: a strict theology, elders, and no music, only hymn-tunes); it is true that Homer allows Athena to do charming conjuring tricks, like turning herself into a swallow, and that he obviously relishes the scandalous tale of Ares and Aphrodite, neither of which would have gone down well in Geneva. But his Mediterranean mind could easily combine such things with the serious idea that the gods, collectively, prefigure something that we could call a world order, and it is within such a framework, or against such a background, that he constructs his plot. This, ultimately, is the reason why it feels so different from mine: mine implies no such background.

This does not in the least mean that Homer was preaching a doctrine or being theological, still less trying to "advance thought"; the mere fact that such a divine governance is so completely taken for granted throughout the poem shows that it was part of what [Francis] Cornford called the "circumambient atmosphere," shared by poet and listeners alike. It is in fact implicit in the ternary structure: the undeserved misfortunes of Odysseus, the disorder in Ithaca, and the concern of the gods thereat are all put fairly and squarely before us in the first few books because these are ultimately what the poem is about. Homer's is not a world in which *anything* can happen; it is one in which certain things *will* happen, even if we have to wait for a long time: of course the gods are not indifferent to lawlessness and disorder. We are bound to assume that Homer's audiences not only agreed with this but also accepted it as a natural basis for a serious poem; otherwise we should have to assume something else which is surely unlikely, that they were as much puzzled or disappointed with some aspects of the poem as some of its later readers have been.

Having considered Homer's σύστασις τῶν πραγμάτων, his plot, assisted, I hope, by the consideration of a very different arrangement of the same facts, we will open the refrigerator in which we left certain doubts or difficulties.

To my scientific friend, as to many others, including perhaps Longinus, the help given by Athena to Odysseus and Telemachus in the fight was matter for regret: Odysseus is the hero, and he would have been more of a hero without the divine aid that caused the Suitors' weapons to fly askew. From an un-Hellenic point of view, yes; from Homer's, no. From his, an Odysseus who should conquer without divine aid would be nearly meaningless; he would lack a certain seriousness, a certain public stature. What is at stake for Homer is rather more than the heroic triumph of his Odysseus; behind this, or rather *in* this, there is the triumph of Order over Disorder. That is something to which the gods are not indifferent; something that concerns any member of human society—which is the reason why I have just spoken of the "public" stature of the hero. Athena's help is essential to the poem. But if so, why is the heroism of Odysseus necessary? Why *both?* Briefly, because the maxim *Do it yourself* never commended itself to Olympus. "The god" did not stop Xerxes with a thunderbolt; in Aeschylus's recreation of the war, the Persians are already ruined by the courage and intelligence of the Greeks and by certain natural causes before the god openly declares his interest by freezing the Strymon. Orestes, in the *Choephori,* is not only directly commanded by Apollo; he also has his own commanding private reasons. It is the standard conception. We should not fail to notice that at book 13, lines 375f., although Athena promises her help to Odysseus, she leaves it to him to devise the means. The world of these poets is not really a world of magic, even though Athena can become a bird or appear to Telemachus as Mentes or Mentor: indeed, when she does choose to appear as one of these wise and intelligent men, it is noticeable that oftener than not what she says is no more than what he might have said; but the fact that it is Athena, not Mentes or Mentor, who says it gives to the advice a certain resonance: it matters nothing to the mechanics of the plot, but it does make the incident somewhat more than a detail in a purely personal story. Athena may have her "special means of transport," namely golden and imperishable sandals, and a "special weapon," accurately described: a great, heavy spear with a blade of sharp bronze, but not on this account does she cease to embody a perfectly clear moral idea. In the *Iliad* a god will show his, or her, power through a Diomedes or Hector—but these had power to start with; a god never magically transforms and uses a nonentity. A god could "help" such a man as Thersites only by making him, as we too might say, supernaturally ugly and vulgar. It is a poetic and vividly imagined world, but not an irrational one. The really irrational world, in which men cowered in bewilderment before discordant demons, did not arrive (as we have seen) [elsewhere] until the fifth century—and in Athens. In Homer, men and gods are in a real sense partners, μεταίτιοι, as Aeschylus remarked, in a forgetful moment. Odysseus's victory without Athena would have been romantic and un-Hellenic because not significant of anything in particular, but no more un-Hellenic than would be Athena's without Odysseus.

We will move on to Longinus's Comedy of Manners, and to the idea that the whole theme of the Suitors falls below epic standards of dignity.

To be fair to Homer, we might first remind ourselves of a subsidiary point. In a rich country, the United States for instance, food and drink do not have the same status as in a poor country like Greece, where the gods are more grudging. Wastefulness was moral obliquity, not an economic virtue. But apart from this, in his handling of the Suitors Homer works two ideas for all he is worth, and Longinus appears to have taken neither into account. One is their moral violence, on which Homer insists more and more as the poem goes on: they are ill-mannered, wasteful, plunderers of another man's wealth, loose-living, and finally plotters of murder, and, in the case of Antinous, of usurpation. All this is brought to a climax that is by no means undramatic when Athena, taking the form of Mentor, comes to Odysseus's help in the fight. Agelaus threatens him (her): "Mentor, keep out of the way. We are going to kill these two men, the father and the son. Then we shall kill you as well; we shall confiscate your estate too, and reduce your family to beggary and shame." The fool does not know, of course, that he is talking to a goddess; even so, it is hardly Comedy of Manners.

The second idea is one that would not perhaps naturally impose itself on a critic living under the Roman Empire. As we have seen, Homer's plot, unlike mine, has a political reference, provided that we use the word "political" in its wide Greek sense. Homer, of course, does not make much fuss about this; as he was a Greek, composing for Greeks, there was no reason why he should; but there are several passages that do not make the degree of sense that we expect of a great poet until we realise that the political framework is present to Homer's mind, whether consciously or quite unconsciously. It does something, perhaps quite a lot, to explain his structure.

First of all, it goes without saying that Odysseus is always the good, wise, and just king, and this is more than a simple characterising of the hero. A picture of such a king is given (as it happens) by Odysseus himself, in a speech that he makes to Penelope (19.106ff.), in which he represents her as the queenly counterpart. He says, in E. V. Rieu's translation:

> Your fame has reached to Heaven itself, like that of some perfect king, who rules over a populous and mighty state with the fear of the gods in his heart, and he upholds the right. Therefore the dark soil yields its wheat and barley, and the trees are laden with ripe fruit, the sheep never fail to bring forth their lambs nor the sea to provide its fish, all because of his wise government; and his people prosper under him.

We notice the same assumption—unless indeed we should say, the same imagery—as in Aeschylus: *Dike,* order, is indivisible; the moral, physical and (here) economic worlds are one. So in the *Eumenides* (ll. 930f.) Athena says of the Erinyes, as the ministers of Dike, that it is their function to order everything for mortals: πάντα γὰρ αὗται τὰ κατ᾽ ἀνθρώπους ἔλαχον διέπειν. Accordingly they invoke upon Attica fruitfulness and wealth, the implied condition being (ll. 1018ff.) that the Athenians revere the Erinyes, the defenders of Dike. The same feeling underlies the long prayer in the *Supplices* (ll. 625ff.): because Argos has chosen to reverence Zeus, Hikesios the chorus prays that the city may be free of war and pestilence, that its crops may be abundant and its cattle fertile. It pervades too Homer's description of Scheria: the people are just, generous, and god-fearing, and (or therefore?) everything is orderly and beautiful; the fruit trees bear at every time of the year. Under the government of a just king "the sheep never fail to bring forth their lambs nor the sea to provide its fish"; and such a king was Odysseus. Ἀδικία, lawlessness, is not a moral phenomenon only.

But in Ithaca, order and government are in abeyance: this is implied throughout. For nineteen years the king has been absent; his son, at the beginning of the poem, is a mere lad, quite helpless; Laertes has given up and gone to his vineyard on the hillside (1.188ff.); even Penelope laments that her troubles have caused her to neglect her duties toward guests, beggars, and messengers who have come on public business (19.133ff.). The royal line is in danger of extinction. Antinous admits (1.386f.) that Telemachus is the natural successor, though Eurymachus at once hints that another might be chosen; but in any case the Suitors are planning to murder him. In the end, when Eurymachus turns king's evidence, hoping to save his own life, he asserts what we can well believe, that Antinous was the ringleader, anxious not so much to marry Penelope as to make himself king (22.48ff.). All this intelligibly connects itself with several notable features of the poem, and they in turn with each other.

We saw that much of the first four books can be accused of having little organic connexion with the rest of the poem, however delightful it may be in itself. But, as many have pointed out, the episode of Telemachus's journey, instigated by Athena, had an ulterior purpose, and one that Athena declares more than once, namely that Telemachus should win renown. It is the poet's way of making the helpless lad grow up; so that at the end of the poem, although it is only thirty-seven days distant counting by the calendar, he is a mere lad no longer, but a young hero, one who can stand valiantly by his father's side, his destined and worthy successor. The real point, of course, is not what happens to Telemachus as if he were a real person, but what happens to our conception of Telemachus as the poem goes on. At his first meeting with Athena, when she is Mentes, he is simply a charming, well-mannered boy. Mentes-Athena tells him that his own qualities and parentage are such that surely his house will continue to be glorious; he can say in answer only that his father is dead, his property being wasted, and he himself likely to be killed. It is Athena-Mentes who urges him to *do* something: to call an Assembly, and to undertake the journey.

During the journey, two things happen to Telemachus—that is, to our conception of Telemachus: he gains in poise, and he gains in stature. At book 3, lines 21ff., he contemplates with alarm the prospect of accosting the great Nestor, but Athena, who is now Mentor, reassures him: he has his native wit, and if that fails, the gods will inspire him. From that moment he speaks to the great with confidence and dignity. Equally important is that the great accept him instantly, both as the son of the renowned Odysseus and on his own obvious merits. Even before the journey, but after his talk with Athena-Mentes, he spoke to Penelope with a new authority that took her aback (1.356ff.); then he firmly told the Suitors, to their surprise, that he intended to be master in his own house and would be willing to succeed Odysseus as king. Towards the end of book 4, Penelope laments that he, a mere boy, should have gone into such danger; when we see him home again, he is much more than a boy: at book 20, lines 266ff. and 304ff. he speaks with great authority to the Suitors, and at book 17, line 45, very firmly to his mother. On each occasion, Homer tells us, his behaviour caused astonishment. We moderns know that a young gentleman should not speak like this to his mother, but how did Homer's audiences respond? With the reflection, I suspect, that under Athena's guidance Telemachus is becoming quite kingly. It is perhaps no accident that in this part of the poem Homer twice makes him improve on a course of action proposed, the one by Eumaeus and the other by Odysseus himself (ll. 146ff. and 308ff.).

The whole episode then, leisurely and delightful though it is, has its close relationship with the rest of the poem; but what about the abortive meeting of the Assembly? It is easy to say that it does nothing to advance the action; one can say the same of the Herald scene in the *Agamemnon,* if one has not understood the play; but in each case the episode does a great deal for the composition and the idea that is shaping it.

Anyone who is disposed to regard this part of book 2 as an interpolation should consider two facts. It is already foreshadowed by Athena at book 1, lines 272ff., so that the two passages stand or fall together; and there is a significant repetition of the same theme at book 16, lines 376ff., when Antinous has just returned from his unsuccessful ambush. He is now taking Telemachus very seriously indeed, and openly warns the others that the time has come to dispose of him. He is dangerous, says Antinous; he may summon an Assembly and denounce us; we may find ourselves banished, for the people now are regarding us with disfavour—a fact for which we must, and easily can, take the speaker's own word. Here, the point is clear enough: what happens to the Suitors is so much more decisive than what Antinous feared: they are not banished but put to death; and not by order of any Assembly, but by Odysseus himself. If Homer found some use in one passage for the idea of an Assembly, he may have found it in two. Perhaps the first is worth looking at in detail.

It is on Athena's prompting that Telemachus summons the meeting. Old Aegyptius opens the discussion: "This is the first time that we have been called together since Odysseus left for Troy. What is the reason? Is the army returning? Is an enemy approaching? Is it something that concerns the public welfare?" Such indeed it is, as we soon learn, even though at first it may seem to be only a private matter.

In response to Aegyptius Telemachus comes forward: in the names of Zeus and Themis (Right) he challenges Ithaca to protect his house from unlawful spoliation. Antinous, in answer, makes an impossible demand. Again Telemachus invokes Zeus—and at once two eagles appear in the sky and hover above the meeting. Haliserthes can read the omen: unless the Suitors give way at once, vengeance will come upon them. The next speaker, contemptuous and defiant, is Eurymachus. He does not believe in birds, nor in justice or moderation either. Finally, Telemachus demands that a ship be given him at least, in order that he may find out, if he can, whether his father is alive or dead; if dead, he will give his mother to a new husband.

Then Mentor rises; he makes a speech that may explain to us why it was his form that Athena chose to assume. He denounces, not so much the Suitors, who are indulging their wickedness (he says) at the risk of their own lives, as the rest of Ithaca, which is doing nothing to stop them. The last speaker, Leiocritus, is another of the Suitors. He defies Mentor, the rest of Ithaca, and Odysseus himself, should he return. He does however suggest that Telemachus should have a ship, though with the sneer that it will be a long time before he sails from Ithaca.

So the Assembly breaks up; and since in the event it is Athena who provides the ship, despite the Suitors, it is understandable if one or two literally-minded critics have found the whole episode a waste of their time. But we should remember that all this was written in Greek, for Greeks. There was a period in English literature too when the connexion between religion, morality, and politics was both close and obvious; it did not long survive Shakespeare, and when we today meet it in Shakespeare, as often as not we fail to see it. The fact that this Assembly accomplishes nothing is the whole point. In the first book we saw the lawless behaviour of the Suitors within the palace, with Telemachus unable to check it. What book 2 does for the poem is to bring the lawlessness out of the seclusion of the palace and put it upon the public stage: it is not a Greek idea that ἀδικία, lawlessness, is a matter only of private conduct and consequence. Telemachus challenges the polis to deal with it, and the polis either cannot or will not. Aegyptius asked: "Or is it something that concerns the public welfare?" But of course it is: what was the polis for, if not to see justice done between man and man? But in the absence of Odysseus the King, public order has broken down; the Assembly has not even met. Zeus sends two warning eagles to signify his displeasure.

It all coheres intelligibly. In Homer's *Odyssey,* in contrast with mine, more is at stake than the return and triumph of the hero. There is the question, expressly raised by Athena, if the gods are content that disorder should prevail unchecked; there is the constant picture of Odysseus as the good king, and for that matter of Penelope as the virtuous queen, contrasted so often with Clytemnestra; there is the moral disorder in the palace; there is its counterpart, the breakdown of public justice in Ithaca, both crying out for the return of the king and the reassertion of authority. It was this wide frame of reference that made the ternary form inevitable: at the outset Homer needed to show us what is at stake.

All this, as it seems to me, makes quite impossible the idea, accepted by several scholars, that Homer's poem ended at book 23, line 296, with the reunion of Odysseus and Penelope. The reason why this is impossible is that it would be the perfect ending for my *Odyssey,* and if it is right for mine, it must be wrong for Homer's. Certainly, before we can feel sure that the whole of book 24 is Homer's work there is much philological and other evidence to consider, but if Homer did not compose it as it stands, the composer was surely working on Homer's own foundations. It is not merely that the idea of countervengeance has been raised twice already, once by Odysseus to Athena (20.36f.) and once by Odysseus to Telemachus (23.117ff.): obviously, an interpolator of book 24 could be clever enough to interpolate these passages too, by way of preparation. One could indeed maintain, rightly, that a countervengeance, or something like it, is implied in what Antinous said in his remark (quoted above) about a possible meeting of the Assembly; but the major point is that the existence and the well-being of the body politic is implied throughout the poem—implied rather than insisted on, for why should Homer insist upon something that any Greek audience would take for granted? As Telemachus brought his private wrongs upon the public stage, to be recognised by Mentor, not to mention Zeus, as a grave public matter, so it is natural, even inevitable, that Odysseus's personal reassertion of justice, within his own house, should have its public counterpart. The palace may have been purified by sulphur, but Ithaca, too, needs something of a purification—at least, a reassertion of authority and order. In any case, no Greek audience could think that the tale had reached its conclusion in a bedroom, when over a hundred young men of Ithaca were lying dead just outside the house. The old Laertes is, surely, using words that Homer wrote for him, when he cries: "Dear gods! What a day to warm my heart! My son and grandson are competing in valour." The king, so long absent, has had his just vengeance and is ready, with his son, to quell countervengeance. But the end is to be conciliation and peace, and it will be strange if Athena is not there to bring it about.

But it may be said: "This is all very well, but among these philosophic generalities where does Nausicaa come in, and the horrible Laestrygonians, Argus the faithful hound, and all the rest? What do they contribute to a supposed theme of order prevailing over disorder?"

So far as I can see, nothing at all—but the question is misconceived. It is understandable if a modern reader should resist, almost instinctively, the attribution of serious thought about the universe to Homer, even to the tragic poets, except perhaps Euripides. These men, we think (rightly) were poets; they were essentially imaginative, creative; we must enjoy them, quite simply, for what they were, not look into their work for what is not there. Hence my own question: But what about Nausicaa? However, the facts are, as it seems to me, decisive; if we feel a difficulty, the explanation is straightforward: we are unconsciously transferring to a different age assumptions based on our own. We ourselves have had no direct experience of a culture that is intelligent enough to produce great poetry but has not developed prose as a medium of communication, except on the everyday level. It may to us seem axiomatic: if no prose, then no sustained thinking; brilliant imaginative insights, yes, but the serious use of the mind as an intellectual instrument did not begin until the time of Thales.

The conclusion is not valid; the existence of conscious mental activity in relation to (say) the nature of the universe, or of human society, may not be simply equated with the existence of prose; it may be the case—and I think evidently is—that intelligent reflection, what I have just called the serious use of the mind, was always there, though in a simple form; that what called for the use of prose was the desire not merely to state the results of thought (for which poetry is a perfectly satisfactory medium) but to question and demonstrate them, and to carry thought still further. In fact, is it not the great difference between Homer's *Odyssey* and mine, poems presumed to be alike in many respects, that Homer's is intelligent, serious, responsible, while mine is not? Mine, surely, would strike a Homeric audience as second-rate, rather empty, in comparison with Homer's. Each (we will presume) has its direct and passionate observation of persons and things, each gives delight and excitement— mine, indeed, rather more excitement than Homer's—but mine restricts itself to a small corner of human experience; it silently assumes, as Homer's does not, that major things like the governance of the universe and the well-being of human society may be neglected. A stranger to our culture might conclude from my poem that ours is a superficial and irresponsible society; he would of course be wrong, not realising that what is serious in our culture does not find expression in our romantic tales but elsewhere—in philosophy, religion, science. Homeric culture had no "elsewhere," so that it is the opposite error to which we are exposed: that of being incredulous when, in what we take to be a work of pure imagination, we are confronted with a serious and consistent concern with certain important moral and political matters. We have forgotten that poetry was the one medium of public communication: no prose, no Church, only poetry; or, if we do not forget it, we fail to work out the implications.

Moreover, we speak, reasonably, of "progress" in thought and culture and then deceive ourselves by our own metaphor, thinking of progress as a linear movement, from the primitive to the advanced. So do we fall into the absurdity of saying either that Aeschylus was nearly as "advanced" as Plato, or "backward" in comparison with Xenophanes—Homer of course being very much in the rear. We should think of the progress as being radial rather than linear; advances are made in various directions from a common centre. This enables us to give a reasonable explanation of the fact that the great tragic poets—Aeschylus, Sophocles, Shakespeare, the poet of the *Iliad*—obstinately deal with the same obstinate material, and in much the same way. They are at the centre, where *backwards* and *forwards* are words without meaning. Progress in this connexion—the discovery of more powerful mental techniques, the acquisition of more and more knowledge—is a matter of increasing specialisation, of advancing from the centre in one direction or in another. Herodotus's *Historia* is an interesting illustration. In reading Herodotus we have sometimes to remind ourselves what the word "historia" meant to him: "enquiries," "researches." In his work, history, geography, and anthropology have just separated out from epic (though without completely cutting the umbilical cord), but have not yet become distinct from each other, and they have not said good-bye to the religious and moral interpretation of things. In our day the radial movement has gone so far that a modern work of sociology will be full of statistics and graphs and no doubt of wisdom, but may well be hardly within shouting distance of theology or ethics, while if it contained a lively sketch of two men in a pub discussing the 3.30 we should feel a certain incongruity. Yet what could be more "social" than that?

In Homeric society, mental activity had hardly begun this radial movement towards remote and far separated points—which is not the same as saying that mental activity did not exist. The circle was still very small; therefore what it contained was all in close and natural contact.

We will notice presently that Homer brings Athena, no less, into a Homeric equivalent of a public house brawl, and we must assume that his audiences were neither shocked nor bewildered. That which was destined, in the long course of time, to become scientific and abstract was still very close to the concrete. Therefore the world of Homer's poem is more complete, more solid, than the world of my *Odyssey:* my poem, by implication, leaves out so much, but Homer's, instinctively, keeps in touch with the whole of his world. The world of my poem extends from the Laestrygonians at one end to Nausicaa at the other, and there it stops, abruptly; Homer's goes on, for it includes a concern for Justice and for the foundations of human society—just as real and natural to him as pirates and a faithful hound—and it includes the gods; and the gods do not inhabit some Platonic otherworld, but a world that makes a continuum with ours.

Here too there is need for caution, lest we suppose that the presence of the primitive excludes the possibility, not of the advanced, but of what was destined to become the advanced.

The gods, we might say, live just over the brow of the hill from us: how much further their region extends, who can say? Yet it too seems to have, on the far side, its boundary: Necessity, or Moira (Apportionment), for the gods too inhabit a world that they did not create but inherited. Although their region has in it terror, faery, and a streak of comedy too, it is to a large extent an extrapolation of our region: what happens here, whether a single event of an unusual kind, like an earthquake, or a general tendency, has its direct or its ultimate explanation in something that happens over the brow of the hill. Many things befall us which are inexplicable or cruel; therefore the gods are, or can be, cruel or capricious. The loyal Philoetius, when he meets Odysseus in the guise of a beggar, cries: "Father Zeus! how cruel you are! You caused us to be born, yet you deal out to us misery and suffering." The cruelty of the gods emerges as an explanation of something that happens with fair regularity. So too Eurycleia, full of her great news, runs upstairs to tell Penelope that Odysseus has not only returned but has also killed the Suitors; and Penelope says: "It cannot be true. Odysseus is dead. The Suitors must have been killed by one of the gods, unable to bear their wickedness any longer." As we know, she is half wrong, half right. *Quod ubique, quod semper* shows the hand of a god; their presence throughout classical Greek poetry serves as a philosophic enlargement of the human world. The poets, from Homer to Sophocles, were really saying, "This is how the world works"—with the unspoken rider: "So that we had better take care." The theology of the philosophers, as we argued above, really was a "theology"; they were not extrapolating.

In the amalgam that we know as Homeric religion there are of course many primitive elements that had no future, but these in no way preclude the presence of other elements that had a very distinguished future indeed: natural philosophy, obviously, is rooted in this idea of generality, and this idea is as consciously present in Homer's poem as it is absent from mine. Homer, just like the tragic poets, though less consistently, interweaves divine action with the human because, or when, he is seeing the human action in its general or universal aspect; what we see as a law or a general principle, he will represent as the act of a god. Early religion was more than primitivism, more than piety, though it comprised both; it contained also that element which was to grow into philosophy and science. In illustration, we will notice the way in which Homer describes an impromptu boxing match; this will bring us back at last to our question about Nausicaa.

The story begins with what is clearly a traditional joke—like the one several times repeated in the poem: "How did you reach Ithaca? Not on foot, I suppose?" The beggar's real name was Arnaeus, but they called him Irus, because he was always running messages for people. Irus, an insolent bully, picks a quarrel with Odysseus, himself in the guise of a beggar, and challenges him to a fight. This quarrel by the door catches the attention of the young gentlemen; Antinous is enchanted at the idea of a fight between a couple of beggars, and proposes that they should make a regular match of it: the winner shall take his pick of the black puddings that are roasting, and shall sit down to dinner with the company, like a real gentleman. All agree; Odysseus is helpfully cunning, and Telemachus intervenes to assure the beggar of a fair fight. When he strips for action all are astonished at his physique. Irus is panic-stricken, and only the direst threats of Antinous persuade him not to turn tail. Odysseus looks at his man wondering whether or not to kill him but thinks it wiser to let him off lightly; therefore he merely smashes in the side of his face, to the intense delight of the Suitors. Then he drags Irus out by one leg, props him up against a wall, gives him his stick, and tells him to squat there and keep the dogs and pigs out. The laughing Suitors warmly congratulate the winner; Antinous gives him a large pudding; Amphinomus gives him two loaves and with all courtesy drinks to his health and future success.—It is a brilliant piece of descriptive writing, amusing, sharp, and clear, with no fuzzy edges, and with no philosophic nonsense in it.

But I have cheated. I have narrated the story as it would appear in my *Odyssey,* and in one particular Homer tells it differently: even in a story of this kind he must needs make Athena interfere, to increase Odysseus's stature for the fight. Could anything be more unnecessary, even on Homer's own showing? We need no assurance that the great Odysseus, victor in many a stern fight before Troy, is well able even in his present guise to stand up to a beggar, but Homer actually introduces Irus with the remark that he had great bulk but little strength or endurance, and when Odysseus throws off his rags, his physique already impresses the Suitors, before Athena magnifies it. Perhaps we murmur to ourselves: "Traditional divine machinery," which, being interpreted, means: "Take no notice of it; think it away, and enjoy the story for its own sake." Treat the whole story, in fact, as it will be treated in my poem, where it will be only a brilliant bit of naturalism. But it is Homer's audience that we must think of. How will they have taken it? Are we to suppose that they were so anaesthetised by tradition that they would take no special notice of Athena's intervention in such a scene?

Our question is answered by the sequel. Homer continues by reporting some observations made privately by Odysseus to the courteous Amphinomus: "Man is a helpless creature! He has to take what the gods send. Look at me, for instance. I was born in a good position, yet I must needs take to the lawless life—and this is the result. Now, look at these Suitors, just as lawless. The man they are robbing and insulting is very soon coming back. . . . I drink to your health, Sir, and I hope that when he comes back you will be safely at home, for there will certainly be bloodshed." Amphinomus took the gold cup from Odysseus's hand and went back to his seat, much perturbed. But this did not save him, for Athena had marked him down to be killed by a spear thrown by Telemachus.—We feel sorry for Amphinomus, as Homer clearly did, but he had touched pitch, and God is no respecter of persons.

But Homer has not yet finished with his vivid and amusing story of the boxing match. A little later in book 18 Penelope chides Telemachus that he had allowed the Suitors to insult one who, though a beggar, was their guest. He replies, in T. E. Lawrence's translation:

> I cannot order all things according to reason, for those men's wicked imaginings pull me hither and thither, and I get help from none. Still, this brawl between Irus and our guest did not end in the least as the Suitors wished, for the stranger proved the doughtier. O Zeus and Apollo! would that these

Suitors in our palace might every one lie vanquished in house
or court with hanging head asprawl, as Irus now squats by
the precinct gates, not able to stand upright or make off home
(wherever home may be) because his limbs are all abroad.

Perhaps this shows that it was not thoughtlessly, from mere force of
habit, in a traditionally epic spasm, that Homer caused Athena to inter-
vene in order to increase, unnecessarily, the strength of Odysseus for a
fight with a flabby braggart. She intervenes of course in a similar way
on many other occasions, to make him look mean or royal, as may suit
the occasion, just as she takes Telemachus in her special care: this one
instance is instructive partly because the reason for it is so clear, partly
because, for us, it is so obtrusive, yet obviously so natural for Homer
and his audiences. The story of the fight, though it begins with a jest
and continues with such gaiety, reveals itself, if we become solemnly
analytical about it, as a paradigmatic myth. Irus is insolent, as are the
Suitors too; Odysseus quells his insolence, as he will quell theirs; Athena
helps him against Irus as she will help him against them; and the prayer
of Telemachus to Father Zeus and Apollo—one of the many instances of
foreshadowing in this part of the poem—makes it clear how, and why,
we must be continually aware of the divine involvement in the story: the
gods, over the brow of the hill, may do all sorts of different things, but
one thing they certainly do is to hate and punish, in the long run, human
lawlessness, this being a deduction from human experience—aided perhaps by hope.

It may be that we shall come yet a little closer to the mind of both
Homer and his audiences if we notice that he does not do what a maladroit
writer or speaker might do today: he does not first tell his racy story of
the fight, and then, to everybody's embarrassment and slight resentment,
go all solemn and point the moral, during which time we respectfully
lay down our pipes or cigarettes and leave our wine untasted. Homer, in
his religious exercises, is quite unembarrassed; he brings Athena into this
casual brawl as if it were the most natural thing in the world—as, to
him, it evidently was. It is we that have divided the week into Sundays
and ordinary days.

Now, a short while ago, after a passage of moral earnestness, I posed
the apparently awkward question about Nausicaa and the rest, and said
in reply that the question was misconceived. Now we can see the reason.
We today, having considerably extended our mental activity from the
centre in many directions, feel that there is a wide gap between what is,

to us, abstract thought and what are, to us, the immediate and vivid realities of life—boxing matches, black puddings, pirates, and the rest. For Homer and his contemporaries the gap did not exist. Homer composes with a continuous awareness of a world which to him is one: its beauty, perils, wonders, its common things whether lovely or hateful, are no more real to him, and no less real, than its divine inhabitants, who give us what we enjoy and what we suffer, often capriciously but on the whole maintaining certain regular courses. That the sun rises and sets with such regularity shows that a *theos* is there; that insolence and lawlessness usually come to a nasty end shows the same thing. The gods were not a pious, or an intellectual, hypothesis; they were one of the obvious facts of life.

If our redrafting of the *Odyssey* has achieved its purpose, it has vindicated Aristotle's dictum that the most important element in poiesis is the arrangement of the material; and by this is meant not simply giving a more or a less elegant shape to something which in either case remains virtually the same thing, but that the arrangement is itself, in the hands of a good poet, a way of saying what he means, a ground plan, as it were, which underlies and articulates the whole significance of the work. My *Odyssey* "says" one thing; Homer's, something quite different.

We have said that Homer could never have invented my plot; why not? We find a clue in the passage already quoted from Cornford. He was speaking of history, but it seems true of any serious composition: that it is "cast in a mould of conception, whether artistic or philosophical [I myself would add "or both at once"], which, long before the work was even contemplated, was already inwrought into the very structure of the poet's mind"; and this, he says, is no personal matter, for "the mind of every individual . . . is not an insulated compartment, but more like a pool in a continuous medium," since every age has "its scheme of unchallenged and unsuspected presuppositions."

My romantic plot would have been impossible for Homer because it is based on an entirely different set of suppositions, natural enough to ourselves but remote from those of Homer's time. Here we have the reason why to Longinus, my own scientific colleague, and certain other critics, some parts of Homer's structure are weak or puzzling; the structure does not fit the new set of assumptions. Much of it will still make sense and give pleasure, but not all of it. Cornford says finally that this element of thought is always difficult to detect and analyse; but we have seen, I hope, that the responsive study of the poiesis of a great poem can sometimes make a little clearer to us some of the fundamental assumptions of its age, even though they may have been half unconscious and unspoken.

This is true because Homer's audiences—or those of Aeschylus or Sophocles or Shakespeare—will naturally have shared the poet's own "scheme of unchallenged and unsuspected presuppositions," since these are poets who expected to be understood by the general. The point may be obvious, but it is important for this reason: one is sometimes told that if the intended significance of a poem or play is to be revealed only by a long and patient analysis, then what is so revealed must be wrong, since the poet must have expected to be understood, or substantially understood, at once, and the original audience could not possibly have so analysed what it was listening to. The objection would be valid if ideas never changed from one age to another. I have myself been told, as critic: "This interpretation does not accord with one's experience of reading the play." The answer is: "Whose experience? Of a reader in 1960, 1760, 260, or 460 B.C.?"

Unless a poem is eccentric, as these two epics are not, it is central—central to the spirit and ideas of its own time; but having said that, we should not commit the folly of thinking that the poems were composed not by Homer, or by two Homers, but by the Homeric age. We have said that the plot of the *Odyssey* is more than a sign of literary genius—but it certainly *is* a sign of genius, and we have good evidence that it was not devised by the Homeric age. As it happens, Aristotle helps us to imagine what the poem might have been like, written by a second-rate poet. He knew epics written by inferior poets and makes two criticisms of them. Homer, he says, stands alone among poets making each poem a real unity; the others imagined that they could do this if they chose a single hero, like Theseus or Heracles, and narrated what happened to him. The comment implies—what is obviously true of both the *Iliad* and the *Odyssey*—that Homer had a real subject and the others not; that Homer took command of his material, selecting and arranging it for his own clear purpose, while the others allowed their material to command them; it did not really pass through their minds, to be sifted, organised, and made significant, so that what unity their poems had was only external and mechanical.

Aristotle's other criticism, which also sets Homer in a class by himself, is that Homer is the only epic poet who knew how much a *poietes* should say in his own voice, namely as little as possible: "for he writes a short proem and then introduces characters who say or do everything, while the other poets are continually taking a hand themselves, αὐτοὶ δι᾽

ὅλου ἀγωνίζονται. But when a poet speaks in his own person, he is not being a *mimetes*." Homer, having his subject, and acting as master of his material, was able to convey what he meant in and through his medium, like the sculptors of whom we spoke earlier; so to speak, he did his thinking at the drawing board. Weaker poets could not do this; they had to talk, moralise, explain the point. But to do this, Aristotle says, is to fail as an artist; it is to cross the line that divides the mimetes from an Empedocles.

But this affects the other partner, the audience or reader, in a way that we might well consider. The difference between Homer and an inferior poet, in this regard, is clear. Let the composer of a *Heracleid* or a *Theseid* be a reasonably good poet, capable of delightful or exciting effects; nevertheless, the response that he creates in his audience will be less taut, less alive and imaginative, than the response created by Homer; we might say that it will be less constructive. We might take the Irus episode as an illustration. As epic narrative it can reasonably be compared with one of Theocritus's *epyllia:* the great difference, of course, is that while each is entirely delightful in itself, the Theocritean piece is no more than that, and was never intended to be, but Homer's (once we have understood the implications of his poiesis) reaches out beyond itself, as it were, and carries meaning; the listener who is attuned to Homer's art—as the original audiences would be—will find himself thinking about insolence, and the way that the gods have with the insolent. In Theocritus's day the gods were not very effective, and in any case this kind of theme was now assigned to the province of the philosophers, not of the poets. We may also compare Homer's treatment of the episode with the way in which, presumably, it would be handled by one of the more talkative and less mimetic poets. Unlike Homer, he will not have so ordered his material from the start as to involve Athena so closely and intelligibly with the fortunes of Odysseus; he will have begun with the birth of Odysseus, his being wounded on Parnassus, his pretending to be mad, and all the rest of it. He, so we will presume, would tell the story of Irus, perhaps quite as well as Homer, and then, αὐτὸς λέγων, would draw the moral, doing this in his own voice because he lacked Homer's constructive ability to make the point without talking. For the listener, the difference is that Homer's art raises him to a higher level of awareness; his imagination will cooperate with Homer's as it cannot do with the other poet's; and from this it seems to follow that Homer's method, the purely mimetic and artistic, not the didactic, is even didactically much more effective. What it conveys is so much more memorable.

Since we recently mentioned Empedocles and Aristotle's distinction between him and Homer, we might bring him into the present discussion too. From the listener's point of view, what is the difference between Homer, who is a mimetes, and Empedocles, who is not? That they have much in common is obvious—"poetry" for example, but Aristotle's distinction is perfectly valid. No one will imagine that Empedocles's poem invited easy listening or reading; quite the contrary. But it is not a matter of the energy of response that is called for, but of its nature. Both poets make demands on our intelligence, but Homer on the imaginative and constructive side, Empedocles on the intellectual and analytical. Reading Homer, we have to apprehend the significance of a mimesis, as if in pictures; reading Empedocles we would have to comprehend an exposition.

The Homecomings of the Achaeans

Agathe Thornton

The homecomings of the Achaeans after the fall of Troy offered a wealth of material for the epic singer. He might sing of the return of Agamemnon, of Menelaus, of Nestor, of Diomedes, of Odysseus and others. The poet of our *Odyssey* chose to sing the homecoming of Odysseus. But he did not therefore exclude all the others; he worked a number of them into the composition of his poem with various purposes in view. We will consider first the functions fulfilled by these Achaean return-stories; and secondly the manner in which they are told.

The most prominent of the Achaean homecomings throughout the *Odyssey* is that of Agamemnon, which is set into relation to each one of the main actors in the poem: to the Suitors, Telemachus, Odysseus and Penelope.

In his opening speech at the beginning of the divine assembly Zeus speaks pensively of Aegisthus, who was killed by Orestes, son of Agamemnon: "Alas, how mortals blame the gods! For they say that evils come from us. But they themselves also by their own outrageous deeds suffer beyond their destiny, as now Aegisthus has married beyond his destiny the wedded wife of Agamemnon, and killed him himself when he came home, although he knew the steep destruction (that threatened him). For we told him beforehand, sending Hermes, the sharp-sighted Argus-killer, not to kill him, nor to marry his wife: "For vengeance will come for Agamemnon from Orestes, when he has reached manhood and longs for his native land." Thus spoke Hermes. But he did not persuade

From *People and Themes in Homer's* Odyssey. © 1970 by Agathe Thornton. Methuen, 1970.

the mind of Aegisthus, however kindly he was disposed; and now Aegisthus has paid the penalty for it all."

Noble Aegisthus married the absent king's wife, Clytemnestra, seized his kingship, and killed King Agamemnon himself on his return. Agamemnon's son, Orestes, when grown to manhood, came home and killed Aegisthus to avenge his father. The nobles of Ithaca woo the absent king's wife, Penelope. They have every intention of killing Odysseus if he should come home and want to drive them out of his house. Antinous and Eurymachus have in mind to usurp the kingship, as we shall see, and kill Telemachus. When Telemachus has come to be a man, and Odysseus has returned in disguise, the two kill the Suitors in revenge for their evil deeds. The parallelism is unmistakable and has often been pointed out.

Zeus's speech makes a brilliant beginning, precisely because its relevance is not immediately evident. The person of whom Zeus thinks first and foremost is Aegisthus, his criminal actions in spite of forewarnings, and his punishment by death at the hands of Orestes. Why does Homer introduce the homecoming of Agamemnon in this oblique way? Why is Agamemnon himself, counterpart of Odysseus, not in the centre of the story of his return? There are two reasons for this. First, in books 1 and 2, the outrageous actions and intentions of the Suitors are represented, and they are forewarned by the words of Telemachus, by omen and prophecy, just as Aegisthus was forewarned. Zeus's speech leads therefore directly into the action at Ithaca. Secondly, by placing the crimes of Aegisthus and their punishment at the beginning, Homer indicates the moral and religious theme which pervades his *Odyssey:* that outrageous actions are punished by the decree of Zeus. In fact, Zeus's speech is "programmatic," as E. R. Dodds puts it.

This theme is not only worked out in the action of the epic when the Suitors are punished by death, but it is constantly kept to the fore in the characterization of the Suitors. The key words are "insolence" (*hybris*) and "violence" (*bie*). Athene disguised as Mentes, watching the Suitors, says that they "seem to feast in the house with excessive wantonness," perpetrating "much that is disgraceful." When Telemachus addresses the Suitors he calls them "Suitors of my mother, men of insolence and violence." This characterization even crystallizes into formulae. When Antinous, the leading prince among the Suitors, hurls a stool at the beggar Odysseus, even his own associates are taken aback and wonder whether the beggar might be a god in disguise. For "in the likeness of strangers from afar, the gods in various forms wander through the cities watching the wantonness and the 'good and orderly life of men.'" The matter is stated by Odysseus himself when, in reply to Eurymachus's entreaty, he refuses to spare the Suitors; not for any gifts whatever would he stop his hand from slaying "until the Suitors had paid the penalty for all their transgression," and Eurycleia, exulting over the bodies of the Suitors, is checked by Odysseus, who realizes that the Suitors' death is brought about by the gods and their own evil deeds, and that they owe their shameful end to their own "wilful folly." Further bloodshed is prevented by Zeus, who causes the kinsfolk of the dead Suitors to "forget the killing of their sons and brothers." This presents a first inkling of a transition from the endlessly destructive justice of kin blood-vengeance to a more humane justice of the gods, as Hommel has shown, who connects this with the mercy of Athene at the end of Aeschylus's *Eumenides*.

Zeus's speech about Aegisthus states then the religious and ethical theme of divine justice worked out in the *Odyssey* in the actions and fate of the Suitors.

The tale of Agamemnon's homecoming ends in young Orestes slaying Aegisthus, the murderer of his father. Our poet has used this part of the story in relation to Telemachus: Orestes, the famous avenger of his father, is set as a glorious example before Telemachus by Athene and by Nestor in order to rouse him to action. This is well known, and needs no further explanation.

Agamemnon himself is brought into relation with Odysseus and indirectly with Penelope. In the Underworld the two heroes meet. Agamemnon describes his death at the hand of Aegisthus and Clytemnestra's betrayal; and then, speaking out of his own experience, warns Odysseus not to trust Penelope, however sensible she is, and not to return to his place openly but in secret.

When Athene and Odysseus meet again for the first time after Odysseus's arrival on Ithaca, Athene tells Odysseus about the Suitors in the palace, and he replies that he would have perished in the same evil fashion as Agamemnon, had the goddess not told him everything. The outcome is of course that Athene turns Odysseus into an old beggar so that he may be unrecognizable and return home in concealment as Agamemnon had suggested.

Finally the lots of Agamemnon, Achilles, the Suitors and indirectly Odysseus are brought together in the second Underworld scene at the beginning of the last book of the epic. This scene needs detailed interpretation as it has not been understood.

The second Underworld scene is a carefully constructed whole. It is introduced by Hermes guiding the spirits of the dead Suitors from the palace at Ithaca down to the asphodel fields of the dead. Hermes is in this scene a guide of souls. He is also a god of sleep and waking, because he is described as "charming the eyes of men with his staff" and waking them from sleep. He is a god of sleep among the Phaeacians, who make to him the last libation in the day when they are on the point of going to bed. Sleep and Death are brothers in the *Iliad;* and they together carry the body of slain Sarpedon to Lycia at Zeus's command, being called "swift guides" or "conductors." Here it is of course the body, and not the spirit, that is carried off after death; and Sarpedon, a son of Zeus, is a special case. But what is plain is the close conjunction of function between death and sleep in Homeric thought. Hermes as god of sleep and guide of the dead is firmly embedded in this context. While most of the time the spirits of the dead leave their bodies and go to Hades without a guide, apart from Hermes in our passage, the *Keres,* death goddesses or daemons, are twice said to "carry" them off. But there are specific reasons for Hermes to be represented as guide of the Suitors' souls at the beginning of the last book of the *Odyssey.*

This passage is closely linked with the end of the previous book, being both parallel and contrasted. There Athene leads Odysseus, Telemachus, Philoetius and Eumaeus out of the town with the first light already on the earth, but she hides them in night. While the Suitors are led, squeaking like bats that flit about in the inner recesses of a big cave, over a mouldy path at last to where "live the souls, images of those who have become tired," Odysseus and his companions emerge, after the Underworld scene, at the rich well-cultivated farm of Laertes, ready for action. Here, at the end of the epos, Athene and Hermes work in concert, though on parallel lines, as they did at the beginning. In book 1 Athene suggests that, while Hermes should go to Calypso and tell her to release Odysseus, she herself will go to Ithaca and rouse Telemachus. She does so, and Hermes goes to Calypso in book 5. The collaboration of Athene and Hermes seems in fact to be traditional: Heracles was accompanied by Hermes and Athene when he fetched Cerberus from the Underworld.

Furthermore, this journey of the Suitors' spirits into Hades is prepared for earlier. In his uncanny vision of the doomed Suitors, Theoclymenus says: "The forehall is full of ghosts, and the courtyard is full of them, hastening towards the Underworld down below the darkness." When the battle in the palace is finished, the bodies of the slain Suitors lie in a heap, like a pile of fish cast on to the beach: nothing is said about their spirits going to Hades. Later their bodies are shifted from the hall to the porch outside and stacked leaning against each other: again nothing about their spirits. Then, Hermes calls them out and sets them moving with his staff. The god's command is needed to initiate the spirits' departure, since a whole book has passed by since the Suitors' death.

Having arrived on the field of asphodel, Hermes and the spirits of the Suitors "found" Achilles accompanied by Patroclus, Antilochus and Ajax. These four heroes are mentioned together by Nestor as having died before Troy; and in the first Underworld scene Achilles is described as being accompanied by the other three in almost identical lines, "And close came the spirit of Agamemnon, son of Atreus," accompanied by all those who died with him in the house of Aegisthus. After a short speech by Achilles, Agamemnon describes to Achilles in great detail the glory and the honours with which he was buried, concluding with a reference to his own wretched death. "Thus they spoke to each other in such a way; and close to them came the Guide of souls, Killer of Argus, leading down the spirits of the Suitors vanquished by Odysseus." The sequence of events is strange here. If it is taken to be chronological, it does not make sense, because Hermes leading the Suitors seems to arrive among the spirits twice over. The clue to the apparent confusion lies in the use of the word "they found" the spirit of Achilles. Cunliffe gives as one shade of meaning of this verb "to find or come upon in a specified place or condition or doing something specified." When in the second book of the *Iliad* everyone was rushing to the ships after Agamemnon's speech, Athene "then found Odysseus, like unto Zeus in intelligence, standing; and he did not touch the black ship with the good rowing benches since grief filled his heart and spirit. Standing close by him owl-eyed Athene spoke to him." Here the verb "found" is followed by over two lines describing Odysseus's attitude and feelings, and then by Athene approaching him and speaking to him. The form of presentation is the same when Iris "finds" Helen, whose weaving and tragic role is described before Iris approaches her, and again when the Ambassadors "find" Achilles, who is described in over five lines as singing to his lyre and having Patroclus sitting beside him, before they step forward and stand in front of him. The common shape of such a scene is then: (1) finding a person, (2) description of the person's state, etc., (3) approaching that person and talking. In the case of Nestor, who was "found" by Agamemnon arranging and exhorting his troops, the second part, that is the description, is seventeen lines long and includes a speech to his men of seven lines.

In the *Odyssey* Telemachus and Pisistratus "found" Menelaus giving a wedding feast for a son and daughter of his to his fellow townsmen. Particulars about the two marriages are given, and about the son born from a slave woman, since Helen had not borne another child after Hermione. After this expansion we return to the wedding feast which is accompanied by a bard's song and the swift circling of two acrobats. Then at last Telemachus and his friend stand at the porch, and contact is made through Eteoneus seeing them. Here the description of Menelaus giving a feast and all the explanation that is added spans over sixteen lines, the explanations in part referring to the past. Finally, in book 5 Calypso found Odysseus "sitting on the beach, and never did his eyes become dry of tears." Through the word "never" the description is immediately widened to comprise the past as well as the present; and the verbs "he used to spend the night" and "he used to look out" (to sea) convey the same. After seven lines of such a description of what he had been doing for a long time, Calypso stands close to him and addresses him.

Our passage in book 24 appears to be shaped on this pattern. Firstly, Hermes and the Suitors "found" the spirit of Achilles and his friends. Thirdly, Hermes leading the Suitors "came close to them." What is in between must be the description of the state in which Hermes finds Achilles. It consists actually of Agamemnon approaching Achilles, who greets him, and a long speech of Agamemnon which exalts Achilles through the detailed description of his funeral before Troy: he is the most glorious of the heroes that have died in the war. So far as chronological time is concerned this meeting between Agamemnon and Achilles would precede Hermes's arrival; the movement into the past between line 15 and line 19 which we who usually think in chronological time must postulate is not noticed by the poet: what matters is that Achilles stands glorified, though a dead spirit, by Agamemnon when Hermes and the dead Suitor Amphimedon come to meet him.

There is another chronological difficulty in connection with this conversation between Achilles and Agamemnon. The actual sequence of events is this: Achilles falls before Troy; Troy is conquered; Agamemnon on his return home is murdered; Odysseus speaks to Agamemnon and Achilles in the Underworld in book 11; Odysseus on his return home kills the Suitors, whose spirits arrive in the Underworld in book 24.

In our passage Agamemnon and Achilles converse, as if Agamemnon had just arrived from the world of the living. Chronologically speaking, this conversation should take place before the events in book 11. We must ask ourselves whether the poet could have had a particular reason for placing this conversation where it is, a reason strong enough to make the awkwardness of sequence of no account.

In order to understand the function of the conversation between Achilles and Agamemnon, it must be considered in relation to the subsequent conversation between Agamemnon and the Suitor Amphimedon.

The connectedness of the two dialogues is formally indicated in two ways. In each part Agamemnon praises a hero as blessed at the beginning of a speech: Achilles first, "blessed son of Peleus," in line 36, and then the absent Odysseus, "blessed son of Laertes," in line 192. Each part is rounded off by the line: "Thus they spoke such things to each other," in the second part one further line being added: "the twain standing in the house of Hades below the covering of the earth." "The twain" refers to Agamemnon and Amphimedon, who have been talking together, Achilles being forgotten. This dual form corresponds to the duals in line 101, "the twain full of amazement then went straight towards him when they saw him." These duals refer to Achilles and Agamemnon, the pair of speakers in the first part. There are then two clearly marked parts with a pair of speakers in each.

In each part the ghost of a dead hero receives someone who approaches him and gives him news about events that have happened on earth since his death. Thus Achilles hears of his funeral from Agamemnon; and Agamemnon hears of the Suitors' fate at the hands of Penelope and Odysseus. In each part the receiving ghost makes a brief speech (11 and 14 lines), and the approaching ghost a long speech (62 and 70/69 lines), Agamemnon's brief reply (11 lines) rounding off the scene.

The content of the two long speeches is the description of Achilles' splendid funeral and the account of the death of the Suitors still lying unburied. The one speaks of the glory of dead Achilles, the other of the winning of life and fame by Odysseus through causing the death of his enemies. In the two long speeches Achilles and Odysseus are set in contrast.

This theme does not appear here for the first time. When Telemachus asks Nestor to tell him of his father's death—he does not believe that he might be alive—Nestor tells him that Ajax is dead, and Achilles, and Patroclus, and his son Antilochus, the same heroes that as spirits surround Achilles in book 24. But he knows nothing about Odysseus. The death of Achilles and the question of whether Odysseus is dead or alive appear side by side. In book 8 the theme of Demodocus's first song is the "Quarrel of Odysseus and Achilles, son of Peleus," a famous song, in which in all probability Achilles spoke on behalf of "might" and

Odysseus on behalf of "guile," the third song being praise of the Wooden Horse which means the victory of Odysseus's guile. Once again Achilles and Odysseus are brought together by the poet: in the Underworld, face to face, Achilles a ghost, but Odysseus a live man. Achilles has with him the same friends who died with him according to Nestor. Odysseus explains his coming to the Underworld, and then he praises Achilles: "In comparison with you, Achilles, no man in the past has ever been very blessed nor will be in future. For formerly when you were alive we Argives honoured you like unto the gods, and now again you rule mightily among the dead, being here. Therefore, though dead, do not grieve, Achilles!" Achilles's answer is well known, that he would rather be the servant of a poor man on the earth than ruler of all the dead below the earth. It is this scene that Homer wants his audience to recall when he once again in book 24 leads us into the Underworld. There Achilles makes no reply when Agamemnon praises him as blessed and describes the marvellous glory of his funeral. But we know that to Achilles sheer life is what he values most, and the description of the great funeral becomes suffused with sadness. In contrast to Achilles, Odysseus does not appear in the Underworld because he is alive, and further he is victorious over his enemies, because he has practised guile more than might. The long train of dead Suitors testifies to his glory.

Between Achilles and Odysseus stands Agamemnon. He calls them both blessed: the one has fame, but is dead; the other is alive, and has fame; but he himself has fought the Trojan War to the end, it is true, but there is no joy in that. He had neither a glorious funeral before Troy, like Achilles; nor is he alive and returned to power at home, like Odysseus. Therefore he concludes by praising Odysseus on account of the good sense and faithfulness of Penelope, so utterly different from Clytemnestra, who killed her husband, Agamemnon.

It is at this point and in book 11 that the story of Agamemnon's fateful return is connected also with Penelope. In book 11 Agamemnon warns Odysseus not, or at least not wholly, to trust Penelope even though he acknowledges the excellence of her mind and character. But at the end of the Underworld scene in book 24 Agamemnon praises Penelope without reserve for her "great virtue" in contrast to the evil deeds of his own wife, Clytemnestra.

To sum up, the meaning of the Underworld scene in book 24 is an assessment of the fates and achievements of Agamemnon, Achilles and Odysseus, an assessment by which Odysseus emerges as the greatest of them all, and that, according to Agamemnon, thanks to Penelope. Here the story of Agamemnon's return together with the death of Achilles before Troy is the sombre background for the glory of Odysseus and Penelope.

The homecomings of Nestor and Menelaus are more restricted both in scope and relevance. Told in books 3 and 4 they give a picture of the wider world of Odysseus, beyond the bounds of Ithaca itself; and so they form a general backdrop to Odysseus's own wanderings which begin with book 5. The function of the homecoming of Menelaus is also more specific. For the climax of his tale is the prophecy of Proteus about Odysseus being a prisoner of Calypso, which leads of course directly to book 5, the book describing Odysseus on Ogygia with Calypso. Furthermore, Menelaus in his home with Helen and looking forward to eternal life in Elysium is, as W. S. Anderson has shown, set in contrast by the poet to Odysseus staying with Calypso, but setting forth on his journey to Ithaca.

In book 1 the bard sings "the grievous homecoming of the Achaeans from Troy which Pallas Athene inflicted on them." This grievous homecoming is described by Nestor in book 3, by Menelaus in book 4, and by Agamemnon in book 11.

In reply to Telemachus's question Nestor tells his tale. When after nine years of war the Achaeans embarked in their ships, "then Zeus planned in his heart a grievous homecoming for the Argives, since they were not all sensible or just. Therefore many of them fulfilled an evil fate arising from the deathly anger of the bright-eyed daughter of a mighty father who caused strife between the two sons of Atreus." Why Athene was angry we are not told. The strife arose in a disorderly drunken assembly held at night: Agamemnon wanted to stay until he had reconciled Athene by sacrifices, but Menelaus wanted to leave. Half of the Achaeans stayed with Agamemnon, the other half, among them Nestor, sailed with Menelaus to Tenedus. Here another quarrel arose, and Odysseus separated off, favouring Agamemnon. Then Nestor fled, recognizing the wrath of the gods, and with him Diomedes. At Lesbus they were overtaken by Menelaus; and they sailed together across the open Aegaean to Geraistus on Euboia. From there Diomedes went to Argus, and Nestor to Pylus with a good wind.

This is the homecoming of Nestor and Diomedes, which Nestor concludes with the words: "Thus I arrived, dear child, without any news, and as far as my own experience goes I know nothing about who of the

Achaeans were saved and who perished." Let us notice here that we have left Agamemnon at Troy, Odysseus at Tenedus, and Menelaus at Geraistus in Euboia.

Nestor then proceeds to tell Telemachus what he has ascertained by hearsay since he returned home. Neoptolemus, Philoctetes, and Idomeneus returned safely; but Agamemnon was killed by Aegisthus and avenged by Orestes, a great example for Telemachus! From this the conversation turns to the state of affairs in Ithaca and back to Agamemnon and Aegisthus, until Telemachus asks Nestor how Agamemnon died, and where Menelaus was at the time, probably wandering about and not in Argus. Nestor agrees at once: if Menelaus had returned home while Aegisthus was alive, Menelaus would have been killed without burial. "For Aegisthus had contrived a great work." While the Achaeans sat before Troy he had won Clytemnestra for himself against her better judgement and had left the bard who was to protect her to die on an empty island. Then he made many sacrifices to the gods, having achieved what he never hoped to achieve. The question of Telemachus about Agamemnon's death is not answered here. But we are told part of the prehistory of that death.

Next Nestor in his tale sets out from Troy once more to go with Menelaus, his close friend. But at sacred Sunium Apollo killed Menelaus's helmsman, so that he was delayed by the burial of his comrade and deprived of an excellent helmsman who might have saved him much trouble. For when he too came to the cape of Maleia Zeus sent a storm which split up his fleet, driving part of it towards Crete where the ships foundered, but the men were saved; the remaining five ships with Menelaus he drove to Egypt, where Menelaus gathered much treasure. In the meantime Aegisthus had ruled at Mycenae for seven years after killing Agamemnon and was killed in the eighth by Orestes. On the very day when Orestes gave to the Argives a funeral feast in honour of Clytemnestra and Aegisthus, Menelaus arrived home with all his treasure. Nestor accordingly advises Telemachus to go and see Menelaus, who would probably have further news.

What is the relationship between the two tales of Nestor? In the first tale, Nestor sets out from Troy with half the Achaeans. At Tenedus Odysseus departs after a quarrel; at Lesbus Menelaus catches up with Nestor and Diomedes, who have fled in haste. They sail together to Euboia. Nestor and Diomedes go home. In the second tale Nestor leaves Troy with Menelaus. At Sunium Menelaus is detained by the death of his helmsman and then is driven to Egypt, from where he returns home.

Each time a complete homecoming is told, that is, a journey from Troy to the homeland. But the two tales are clearly distinguished in that the first tale is told by an eyewitness, Nestor himself, the second from hearsay. The first also represents in some detail the drunken, quarrelsome assembly which caused the scattered return of the Achaeans. The first tale, then, is the homecoming of Nestor with his companion Diomedes, told by Nestor himself. The second tale comprises the prehistory of Agamemnon's death, told from hearsay, which makes us expect a description of Agamemnon's death at some time or other in the poem and the homecoming of Menelaus, also by hearsay, at least from Sunium on. It is noteworthy that in the telling of this homecoming no reference is made back to the first tale: no mention of the quarrel or Odysseus or Diomedes or the details of the journey between Troy and Euboia. But Menelaus and Nestor are taken from Troy straight to Sunium. The second tale is in fact a supplement to or explanation of the first tale without this being made in any way explicit; it is also a continuation since—implicitly at least—Menelaus had been left at Geraistus in Euboia. This method of piecemeal, supplementary narration is characteristically Homeric, as Schadewaldt has pointed out. But it is here complicated by the difficulty of telling parallel sequences of events. This sort of thing is managed without trouble where the parallel events are told briefly, as in book 3 where the contemporaneity of Aegisthus's deeds and Menelaus's wanderings is expressed by *tophra,* but the much more extensive contemporaneous sequences of the homecomings of Nestor (and Diomedes) and of Menelaus (at the beginning with Nestor) are not told as contemporaneous but as two separate sequences without relation to each other.

In book 4 Menelaus tells about his own homecoming, again in two speeches.

Telemachus, full of admiration for Menelaus's wealth, whispers to Pisistratus, and Menelaus overhears his words. He explains how after much suffering and much wandering he brought his treasures home in the eighth year. Expanding on his wanderings, he says that he went to Cyprus, Phoenicia and Egypt, to the Ethiopians, Sidonians, Erembi, and to Libya about which he gives some detail. But during his absence his brother was killed by some man through his wife's deceitfulness. And now Menelaus is sad, mourning those who died before Troy and grieving for Odysseus, who is lost in the unknown. Here we have in fact a further expansion on the homecoming of Menelaus, but it is not told as part of a homecoming. It is told with strict relevance to the situation as an explanation for his great wealth.

The next day Menelaus asks Telemachus what he has come for, and Telemachus asks him for news of his father. Then Menelaus tells him all "that the unerring man of the sea told him." It is unnecessary to retell the story of how Proteus, the ancient many-formed herd of seals, was caught: Menelaus relates what he has lived through himself, and the detail is vivid down to the smells. Enfolded within the Proteus story are the homecomings. For Menelaus asks him whether all the Achaeans whom he and Nestor left behind at Troy had come home safely in their ships. Proteus relates how Ajax, son of Oileus, was drowned by Poseidon for his boastfulness off the Euboian rocks of Gyrae. Then he tells of Agamemnon's homecoming in some detail. A storm carried Agamemnon to the part of the land where Aegisthus lived, but the gods sent him a wind which safely carried him further homewards; and he stepped gladly ashore and kissed his native land. The fact that Agamemnon is almost forced to land by the very house of Aegisthus, but gets safely away, is pointless to us: it indicates a portion of Agamemnon's homecoming which we do not know. Perhaps in this part Agamemnon's falling into the hands of Aegisthus was brought close, but dramatically retarded again. What happened after that is related in detail: the guard who waited a year for the payment of two talents of gold, the ambush of twenty men, the preparation for a banquet, Aegisthus's fetching Agamemnon and killing him at the dinner table, like an ox at the crib, and the death of all the followers of both Agamemnon and Aegisthus. Whether Menelaus will find Aegisthus alive or already killed by Orestes and being buried, is left open. We know the answer already from Nestor's story. Having recovered from his first grief, Menelaus asks about Odysseus and hears about Calypso keeping him a prisoner. Finally Menelaus returns to the river Egypt and makes sacrifices, as Proteus told him to do, and then returns home to his own country.

Ostensibly, Proteus's story is told for the sake of the information which it contains about Odysseus. It is also a rich expansion on Menelaus's time in Egypt already mentioned by Nestor and by Menelaus himself in his earlier speech. It contains also a grievous homecoming of Ajax, son of Oileus; and furthermore what we have been led to expect: the story of Agamemnon's return and death in some detail. Here the story begun by Nestor of how Aegisthus beguiled and won Clytemnestra finds its due completion in the account of Proteus. Let us notice, however, that the voyage of Nestor is told by Nestor himself, the story of Proteus by Menelaus, and the story of Agamemnon is so far told by Nestor and Menelaus, who heard it from others.

In the book of the Underworld, through the mouth of Odysseus, Agamemnon himself describes his death. How Aegisthus together with Clytemnestra invited him to his house and killed him at the dinner table, like an ox at the crib—the simile is repeated from Proteus's description—how his friends lay dead, like pigs slaughtered for a banquet in a rich man's house, how pitifully the dead lay, not on the battlefield, but among mixing bowls and tables laden with food: "and the whole floor was running with blood." Both the picture of the slain in the midst of a banquet and the last half line point forward to the death of the Suitors. The death of Cassandra at Clytemnestra's hands, how Agamemnon died at last, and how Clytemnestra kept away from him are further new details. Clytemnestra was not mentioned in Proteus's account. The most terrible part of Agamemnon's death is told by himself, namely the part that Clytemnestra played in it.

From the point of view of content the Agamemnon passage in book 11 is an expansion on Proteus's tale. What gives it new intensity and power is the fact that it is told by the murdered man himself, as Nestor told of his own voyage, and Menelaus told of his meeting with Proteus himself.

It is great praise for a poet to be told, as Odysseus tells Demodocus, that he sings the fate of the Achaeans like one who was present himself or heard it from an eyewitness. In the tales of the Achaeans' homecomings Homer has aimed at this very immediacy of presentation by putting the most detailed and intense description of events into the mouths of those who experienced them themselves.

The *Odyssey:* Its Shape and Character

C. M. Bowra

The *Odyssey*, like the *Iliad*, begins with an invocation to the Muse:

> Tell, Muse, of the man of many devices, who wandered far
> indeed, when he had sacked the holy citadel of Troy. He saw
> the cities of many men and knew their minds, and many were
> the sorrows which he suffered in his spirit on the sea, when
> he tried to win his own life and the return of his companions.
> But not even so, for all his desire, did he save his companions;
> for they were destroyed by their own insolence, when they ate
> the cattle of the Sun Hyperion; and he robbed them of the day
> of their return. From what point you will, goddess, daughter
> of Zeus, speak to us also.
>
> (1.1–10)

This presents several surprises. Unlike Achilles at the start of the *Iliad*, the hero of the *Odyssey* is not named but called "the man of many devices," which indicates that his story is familiar, and this is confirmed by the last words when the muse is asked to "speak to us also." But the familiar story is outlined in a peculiar way. The fantastic adventures of Odysseus are inadequately, almost deceptively, suggested in the reference to cities and minds; almost the only city seen by him is the capital of Phaeacia, and minds are not what he marks in the Cyclops and other monsters. Next, the emphasis on his struggle to save his own life is fair enough and anticipates some of his bravest efforts, but he hardly does so much to secure the return of his comrades. He looks after them, but he

From *Homer.* © 1972 by the Estate of C. M. Bowra. Duckworth, 1972.

takes risks with their lives, and more than once he is the cause of their loss. Finally, not a word is said about the Suitors and the vengeance on them. They occupy more than half the poem and provide its central theme. The opening lines of the *Odyssey* are much less apt and less relevant than those of the *Iliad*.

Odysseus must have been the subject of many different stories, some of which survive outside the *Odyssey*, and even of the more constant stories there were variations, as we can see from the Homeric text. When Homer announces his theme at the start, he assumes that much will be known about Odysseus, and the special surprises which he has in store are not of the kind to be publicised now. It is enough that he should refer vaguely to the wanderings and the sufferings of Odysseus and that he should hint at his ultimate return home. It is more striking that he makes such a point of the comrades and their untoward doom, and this is more than a passing whim. One of the chief features of the *Odyssey* is that at the crisis of his fortunes Odysseus has to act alone. Calypso can do little to help him, and on Ithaca he has to find what support he can, first from Eumaeus and then from Telemachus. Therefore his comrades must be disposed of, and their eating of the cattle of the sun meets a real need in the story. Because of this Odysseus's last ship is wrecked, and he himself is cast up on Calypso's island. Homer does not actually give false clues, but his clues are a little delusive. His aim is to keep his audience guessing about how he will treat a familiar mass of stories, which none the less have to be selected and remodelled to suit his own taste.

The material of the *Odyssey* differs greatly from that of the *Iliad* and gives it a different character. While the *Iliad* tells of the "glorious doings of men" and is heroic in the sense that heroes struggle against other heroes, the *Odyssey* uses a less specific and less exalted material. Its stories are ultimately fairy tales or folktales, and are unheroic in the sense that the unquestionable hero Odysseus is faced not by his equals but by his inferiors or by monsters. In its own compass it displays two kinds of narrative. Books 1–4 and 13–24 tell the age-old tale of the Wanderer's Return and his vengeance on the Suitors who devour his substance and try to marry his wife. In this there is not much fantasy or marvel. Instead we find what Longinus calls "a comedy of manners" (*On the Sublime*, 9.15). By this he means that it is concerned with the behaviour of human beings at a familiar and not very exalted level, as he himself knew it in the comedies of Menander. So far as it goes, this is fair enough, as is also his judgment on books 5–12, in which he speaks of "a fancy roving in the fabulous and incredible" (ibid., 9.13). The two parts differ greatly in matter, scale, temper and outlook. The second consists of stories so ancient that they seem to have been polished and perfected by constant telling, while the first class, which deals with stories hardly less ancient but of a different kind, has a less confident and less accomplished, even more experimental and more tentative, air.

The *Odyssey* serves in some sense as a sequel to the *Iliad.* No doubt there were many such sequels, especially in the creative heyday of oral song. The tale of Troy had many consequences, and among these were the adventures of Odysseus. In time he became the chief of the surviving heroes, and his return the most famous of many. Once a figure becomes known for certain qualities, appropriate adventures, with which he may originally have had no connexion, are attached to him and marked with his personal imprint. Odysseus seems from the start to have been "wily" and "much-enduring," and stories which turned on wiliness or endurance were annexed to him. The relation of the *Odyssey* to the *Iliad* is obvious throughout. The past in retrospect is seen to have been disastrous, the story of "evil Ilium not to be named" (19.260, 597; 23.19), words which do not occur in the *Iliad* and suggest a shift of attitude towards the Trojan War. At the start of the *Odyssey,* when the gods discuss the fate of Odysseus as he languishes on Calypso's island, they turn at once to the fate of his old comrade, Agamemnon, who has been murdered by his wife and her lover (1.35ff.), and this broaches the topic of what happens to the heroes of Troy. The audience knows all about the Trojan War and can take any reference to it. So now it lies in the background as they hear about Odysseus and Ithaca.

In the *Odyssey* certain characters appear who have played a substantial part in the *Iliad* but need not necessarily play any part in the return of Odysseus. When Telemachus sails off to find news of his father, he visits first Nestor at Pylos and then Menelaus and Helen at Sparta. Nestor is just the same as in the *Iliad,* garrulous, generous, helpful, even wise. Actually he contributes very little to Telemachus's knowledge of his father, and Homer shows a flicker of playful malice when Telemachus, eager to embark on his ship at Pylos and get home, decides to do so without seeing Nestor, since this would waste a lot of time (15.199–201), and sends the young Peisistratus to fix things with him. Menelaus is a less marked personality than Nestor, but he shows the kingly qualities which we expect from him, and especially loyalty to the son of his old friend Odysseus. More striking is Helen, who makes only a few appearances in the *Iliad* but in all of them reveals the pathos of her doom and her desire to escape from it. Her capacity for affection is clear from what she says to Priam (*Iliad*, 3.172), to Hector in his lifetime (*Iliad*, 6.344ff.) and about him after his death (*Iliad*, 24.762ff.). The whole adventure with Paris has been a sorrow and a disaster for her, but she has not been able to avoid it (*Iliad*, 3.399ff.). Now she is back with Menelaus at Sparta, happy and at peace. She recalls without distress episodes from the war, but the scope of her character is revealed when she sees that Menelaus and his guests are distressing themselves with reminiscences, and mixes a drug which she has brought from Egypt and which deadens pain and sorrow (4.219ff.). She has learned from her sufferings, and the tenderness which is already hers in the *Iliad* is turned to new purposes.

Odysseus himself in the *Odyssey* is an enlarged and elaborated version of what he is in the *Iliad*. His main qualities there are cunning and endurance. He keeps his head when others lose theirs, notably after Agamemnon's ill-judged test of the army's morale (*Iliad*, 2.166ff.). He is throughout a notable leader, resourceful and brave. In the *Odyssey*, where he is far longer on the stage, some of his qualities are turned in new directions. First, his cunning is tested in unfamiliar conditions, as in the cave of the Cyclops, where he takes on some qualities of a folk hero and sustains them quite convincingly. Secondly, his need for cunning is enforced by his own recklessness. It is his fault that he is trapped in the cave of the Cyclops, since he has insisted on entering it, and equally it is his fault that he seeks out Circe's dwelling by himself. Thirdly, his abundant appetites, known from his taste for food and drink in the *Iliad*, are extended in the *Odyssey* to living with Circe and with Calypso, not perhaps in entire satisfaction but still competently. Lastly, the warrior of the *Iliad* becomes the returned wanderer of the *Odyssey* and needs all his powers of decision, command and improvisation. These he amply displays. The man who strikes Thersites and kills Dolon is not likely to spare the Suitors or the servants, male and female, who have worked for them. Odysseus in the *Odyssey* is a magnified version of Odysseus in the *Iliad*, but he remains substantially the same man and recognizable in his main being.

Finally, there are in the *Odyssey* two passages where Homer presents ghosts of the dead, and each includes some chief figures of the *Iliad*. At 2.385–567 Odysseus, at the end of the world, summons ghosts with an offering of blood, and among those who appear are Agamemnon, Achilles and Aias. All three have died since the end of the *Iliad*. Agamemnon has been murdered by his wife, in marked contrast with Odysseus, whose faithful Penelope holds out bravely against the Suitors. His story emphasizes the dangers that await those who return from Troy, but sheds no new light on his personality. Aias, in a brief appearance, adds a new dimension to his simple character in the *Iliad,* for in the interval he has killed himself because his honour has been wounded by Odysseus. Odysseus does his best to appease him, but Aias takes no notice and makes no answer. The most striking figure is Achilles, for his words complement by contrast what he says in book 9 when momentarily he rejects the heroic life. Now he knows what he has lost, for he would rather "work on the land as the serf of a man with no property, with no great means of life, than reign over all the perished dead" (2.489–91). His only consolation is to know that his son Neoptolemus is already a stout warrior (2.540). These three ghosts form a link with the *Iliad,* and when Odysseus speaks to them he speaks to his peers, as he does nowhere else in the *Odyssey.*

More mysterious is 24.1–204, where the ghosts of the Suitors are escorted by Hermes to the land of the dead and met by some heroes of the *Iliad,* notably Achilles and Agamemnon. Though the passage is thought to be a later addition, at least it has a part in the whole plan of the *Odyssey.* Achilles hears of his own death and funeral from Agamemnon (24.36ff.); at it the Muses sang and the ceremony is a fitting climax to a heroic life. To this the Suitors present a complete antithesis. Their ignominious deaths are the proper end to their squalid careers. In this passage the poet seems to have aimed at more than one effect. First, when he makes Agamemnon say that Odysseus is indeed fortunate to have a wife like Penelope (24.192ff.) and very unlike Clytaemnestra, he emphasizes a subsidiary theme of the *Odyssey,* but does not gain much by it. Secondly, the parade of the ghosts of Troy, in which Patroclus, Aias and Antilochus are named as well as Achilles and Agamemnon (24.16–17), provides a final curtain for great figures of the *Iliad* and of the heroic age. Their place here recalls them at the end of a long story, and the renewed attention paid to them brings various themes together in a last bow. Thirdly, there is a real contrast between the death and glory of Achilles, immortalized in song and the miserable careers of the Suitors, who are at the other extreme from the true nobility of the heroic ideal. Whoever composed this passage must have felt that the *Odyssey* must be brought into contact with the *Iliad,* and this he did by stressing what real heroes are.

When we look at the structure of the *Odyssey,* books 1–4 look as if they could be omitted by bards who were pressed for time and wished to plunge in medias res with the more thrilling adventures of Odysseus, but this does not mean that these books do not serve a dramatic purpose.

In fact they serve more than one. First, they show the general plight of Ithaca and the particular plight of Penelope in the absence of Odysseus. This is indispensable to any understanding of his difficulties on his return and of the character of the Suitors, from whom he is to exact vengeance. It is bad enough that they should harry his wife and devour his substance and corrupt his servants, but they soon put themselves brutally in the wrong by plotting the death of Telemachus. In this situation everything turns on the possible return of Odysseus. The poet shows how little is known of him, how anticipations of his return vary between irrational hope and not impossible despair. This creates the suspense at which the poet excels. It is to some extent lessened when Telemachus gets news of Odysseus from Menelaus, but it remains vague and unsubstantiated, though omens and portents suggest that something is going to happen. These books build up a growing assurance in the return of Odysseus, and incidentally introduce the other characters with whom he will be associated. The *Odyssey* can be imagined without them, but they add to its range and richness and do much to set its plot to work.

Books 1–4 do more than this. They prepare the way for much that comes later. For instance, Telemachus is cast for a large part, and is not yet ready for it. But he begins to face his responsibilities and to test his powers. His access of courage takes the Suitors by surprise (1.381–82; 2.85–86), and before long they are sufficiently afraid of him to plot his death. By this means he becomes an important participant in the action, and he gives sturdy help in the vengeance. Again, these books anticipate in their manner the dual nature of the *Odyssey*, its element of domestic comedy and its element of fable and fancy. The first is to the fore here, and has a special charm. This manner is unadventurous and unexciting, but its human normality presents a fine contrast with the gluttonous revels and gross manners of the Suitors. Against this are set the stories told by Telemachus's hosts at Sparta, which take us either back to the heroic world of Troy, as when Helen tells how she recognized Odysseus when he came disguised as a beggar to spy in Troy (4.240–64), or forward to the world of marvels, as when Menelaus tells how he tricked Proteus, the old man of the sea, into revealing the fate of Odysseus (4.351ff.). The main notes of the *Odyssey* are struck at the start, and in due course each is taken up to make its contribution to the whole design.

The middle section of the *Odyssey*, books 5–12, has a notably distinctive character. Though its more extravagant actions are told by Odysseus himself, the first part, his departure from Calypso and his arrival and welcome in Phaeacia, are told in the third person with an outstanding objectivity, in which Odysseus emerges in all his gifts and dominates the scene. These books provide a skilful transition to the wonders that follow. The events are not yet marvellous, nor are there any monsters. Odysseus shows his physical powers by swimming in a rough sea for two days and two nights, and his resourcefulness by winning the help of the Phaeacian royal family. Yet Phaeacia is not real in the same sense as Ithaca. The seasons allow crops all the year round; the servants in the palace are made of metal by Hephaestus; the Phaeacians hardly mingle with other peoples and are consciously proud of their singularity; unlike authentic heroes they live not for war but for dance and song. Once Odysseus has arrived and been handsomely welcomed, we are ready to hear of the wilder wonders which he is about to tell. In Phaeacia these seem less improbable than in Ithaca, and the lively entertainment in Phaeacia prepares us for what lies outside the known world. At the start we have even left the sea, but it is soon present again when Odysseus tells his tale.

Even at this stage, and still more in the narrative of Odysseus, it is clear that the poet is familiar with different versions of a tale and has to make his choice between them. This is easy enough when Odysseus meets Nausicaa. The theme of Wanderer meeting the king's daughter is old and widely spread. A less human version is known from Egypt. A man is shipwrecked on an island. He finds it rich in fruit and trees, and is royally entertained, loaded with gifts and given a safe passage home to Egypt. But his hostess is a snake, thirty ells long, and her family is like her. She treats the castaway with much kindness and courtesy; this is a primitive version of the Nausicaa story, which has not yet assumed its fully human character. The episode in the *Odyssey* shows no misfits or oddities, and looks like a complete tale, but it may well have grown from humble origins. What is remarkable is that while Homer hints at a story in which the Wanderer marries the Princess, the Egyptian tale suggests nothing of the kind. So the treatment of Nausicaa by Odysseus has an ancient precedent. In this case variants have been absorbed into a final version, and Homer's choice was forced upon him by Odysseus's destiny to be joined again to Penelope.

In their long and widely scattered careers such tales develop variations, and the poet has to choose between alternatives. This is very much the case with the Cyclops. As the *Odyssey* tells it, the substantial, unchanged element is that the hero and his companion are caught in the cave of a one-eyed cannibal giant, and after suffering losses in their own number blind him and escape. This story occurs in many countries and is clearly primordial. Homer knew more than one version and made his own choice. First, there is the trick by which Odysseus says that his name is "No-man," and so when the Cyclops calls for help and says "No-man is hurting me" (9.408), his friends go away. The trick throve happily in other contexts, but is well in place here. To set the Cyclops among other monsters of his kind makes him more formidable and increases the danger to Odysseus; the trick saves him at a critical point. Second, the Cyclops is blinded with a stake lying in the cave which is not yet ready for use. That is why the Cyclops will not take it with him when he goes out, and Odysseus can use it to blind him. The Cyclops eats his visitors raw after breaking their heads on the floor like puppies (9.289–90). This is perhaps more bestial than to cook them first, and since there is no need for a spit, the stake takes its place. Thirdly, in the escape from the cave there is one version in which Odysseus and his companions kill the ram and the sheep, clothe themselves in their skins, and behave like them as they walk out on all fours. But the Homeric version brings advantages, notably when the ram goes out, with Odysseus under its belly, and we are simultaneously afraid that the Cyclops will catch the escapers and touched by his affectionate words to the ram. Choices between competing versions had to be made, and were, usually with good results.

The episode of Circe, which reads very easily, contains traces of competing versions. She is a witch, daughter of the sun, who lives in a stone palace among woods on an otherwise uninhabited island. This is common form, and suggests her dangerous character. In such stories the adventurer is guided to her by some chance, and behind the story in the *Odyssey* we may discern a stag who did the guiding. Odysseus meets such a stag but kills it and with some effort carries it to his companions for their supper (10.156ff.). Then having seen the palace, he decides to send a party to investigate. He does not go himself or take the lead, but divides his crew into two companies, one of which is chosen by lot to go. This procedure creates suspense and leaves Odysseus free to take action later and remedy the evils that have befallen the first party. This party finds wolves and lions which greet it in a friendly way, and are in fact men transformed by Circe. But this is their only appearance. When the companions are turned back into men from swine, nothing is said about these earlier victims. Their function is to reveal something sinister in Circe's dwelling, and when they have done that, they are forgotten. When Odysseus's companions are turned into swine, we are expressly told that they keep their wits as before (10.240), and this is not usual in this kind of theme, where the witch tends to instil forgetfulness of former lives. We may guess why Homer does what he does. He has already dealt with the theme of forgetfulness in telling of the Lotus-eaters, who forget all about their return home (9.94–97), and the theme is not suitable for repetition. Finally, on his way to Circe Odysseus meets Hermes, who tells him of the danger ahead and gives him a plant, *moly,* to protect him from Circe's spells. The plant is carefully described, and then we hear no more. We do not know how Odysseus uses it, or how it works; what we do know is that Circe's spells have no effect on him. In these ways Homer keeps the episode of Circe simple and circumvents obstacles in the tradition.

In the passage of years a traditional theme may assume new shapes, which are so different that they are really new tales. The *Odyssey* deals twice with the ancient theme of the witch who detains the hero on his return by making him live with her. She need not be malevolent but she hinders his desire to go home. In the *Odyssey* she appears in two quite different forms, as Circe and Calypso. If Circe, who has a ruthless, cruel side, is the Hawk, Calypso is the Concealer, who keeps Odysseus hidden on Ogygia for eight years. Both live alone on remote islands, in circumstances of some beauty. Yet, allowing for this degree of likeness, the differences are great. Circe is subdued by the superior cunning and courage of Odysseus, and after admitting her defeat, welcomes him as her lover; Calypso saves him from the sea after shipwreck and her devotion to him is complete. Circe keeps Odysseus for a year and then releases him without complaint; Calypso keeps him for eight years, hoping to make him immortal but is told by the gods to give him up, which she does unhappily but graciously. Circe at the start has a sinister glamour; there is nothing sinister in Calypso. The two are distinct and distinguishable, but we can see why both are needed. The adventure with Circe is exciting for its own sake and entirely appropriate to the hero on his wanderings; the sojourn with Calypso has much charm and beauty but lacks dramatic variety. It is needed to fill a gap in the story. After his ten years of war at Troy Odysseus is away from home for another ten years before he returns to Ithaca. By the time of his shipwreck and the loss of all his companions only two years have passed, and the remaining eight have to be accounted for. Homer does this by confining him to Calypso's island, where nothing can be heard of him and his fate remains a mystery to his family and his friends, and is almost forgotten by the gods.

Circe begins as a malevolent witch, but once Odysseus has subdued her, she becomes his helper and shows no signs of her sinister past. She then takes up another part which may belong to her original character—

she foretells the future and gives advice about it. That heroes should have this happen is common enough, but Homer seems to have been faced by two traditional characters who prophesy. Circe is one, but she insists that Odysseus should consult the other—the ghost of the seer Tiresias. This is a very ancient theme and bears some resemblance to *Gilgamesh*, where the hero crosses the waters of death to consult Uta-Napishtim. Odysseus sails to the edge of the world and calls up the ghost of Tiresias, who says very little about the immediate future, except in warning him not to eat the cattle of the Sun in Thrinacia (2.104ff.), but gives him a precise forecast of his last days and quiet ending (2.121ff.), with advice on the ritual that will appease Poseidon. We may perhaps assume that in earlier versions Tiresias said more than this, and that his warning about the cattle is only part of a set of warnings and forecasts. But Homer transfers these to Circe. When Odysseus comes back to her, she gives him a careful forecast of the dangers that lie before him (12.37–141). This device keeps Circe still powerful, even if she has reformed her habits, but at the cost of a lengthy prevision of what will come soon afterwards. It all happens according to plan, but lacks the element of surprise.

In books 13–24 we are back in Ithaca and a familiar world. Yet here too the main actions are derived largely from folktale, and old themes exploited with novelty. At some point the Wanderer must be recognized. No doubt there were many versions of this, and the recognition need not all come at once. Homer moves through a series of recognitions, each separate and distinct, and each marking a step forward. The first is when Odysseus, transformed into a shrunken old beggar is for a short time given back his old shape and reveals himself to Telemachus (16.166ff.). Athene makes it possible, and to that degree it is supernatural. What matters is that Odysseus must not start on his vengeance entirely alone, and his obvious companion is his son, who stays with him for the rest of the poem. The second recognition is a stroke of genius. When Odysseus arrives at his palace, he sees lying in his midden outside the gates his dog Argos, whom he trained twenty years before. The dog is neglected and full of ticks, but he wags his tail and drops his ears and struggles towards his old master (17.291–304). Odysseus knows him at once and says a few words about him, and then the dog dies "having seen Odysseus again in the twentieth year" (17.327). This recognition is based on affection and loyalty and conveys swiftly and surely how Odysseus belongs to Ithaca and how deep his roots there are. The third comes when Odysseus has his feet washed by his old nurse, Euryclea. It is dark, and Penelope is sitting in the shadow not far away. The nurse recognizes a scar which Odysseus got long ago on a boar hunt, and is on the point of crying out, when the basin of water is upset and Odysseus puts his hand on her throat and enjoins her silence (19.386ff.). This is the most dramatic of the recognitions, and the one in which the scar, used twice elsewhere, really creates a situation. Through it the recognition by Penelope is postponed until it can be most effective. In the fourth recognition, during the fight in the hall, Odysseus reveals himself to Eumaeus, who accepts his word and, like the nurse, recognizes the scar, but without any exciting reaction (21.207ff.). Fifth is the recognition by Penelope, and this is the most unexpected. The signs that have satisfied others do not satisfy her, and she tries to test the stranger by telling Euryclea to make a bed, but the stranger knows that Penelope and he have their own special, secret bed made out of an olive trunk in the heart of the palace. This is highly appropriate, as Odysseus and Penelope are man and wife and the bed is an intimate sign of it. Finally, Odysseus goes off to see his old father Laertes in the country and identifies himself first by the scar (24.331ff.) and then by knowing the details of Laertes's orchard, which he helped to plant. All these recognitions have a certain simplicity. If the scar does the most work, that is perhaps because it comes from the oldest tradition, while the dog Argos, who needs no sign, looks as if he were Homer's own invention. The accumulation of six recognitions suggests that there were many variants in the tradition and that Homer gave a subordinate purpose to some which might have been of primary importance in earlier versions.

Somewhat different from the recognitions are two events which do not reveal the identity of the Wanderer but show that he is someone remarkable. These are the stringing of the great bow which Odysseus left behind when he went to Troy (21.39), and the exhibition-shot with it through a line of axes planted in the ground. It is conceivable that in earlier versions the two events were alternative and that either of them would suffice to prove who Odysseus is. Nor must we assume that, once the bow had been strung, the slaughter of the Suitors followed immediately. The *Odyssey* finds its climax in the combination of these events, but it is possible that originally neither event served just this purpose. The stringing of the bow may have been no more than a test of the Wanderer's identity, proposed by his wife, who is still not sure of him. So the exhibition-shot may have come from some other context, as when the Suitors compete for marriage with Penelope, and even then Odysseus need not take a part. In its present place it establishes his preeminence, and leaves him with the bow in his hands as an instrument for vengeance.

When a story belongs to a cycle centred on some main point, it may not fit in easily with others in a like position. Tradition is aware of its place, and the poet may feel that he owes it some attention, but it may lead to difficulties and to some awkwardness in his main scheme. This is the case, in the *Odyssey*, with the shroud which Penelope claims to be weaving for Laertes when he dies. She tells the Suitors that when it is finished, she will make her choice among them, but every night she undoes the work of the day, until a point comes when the Suitors catch her at it and know that she is deceiving them (2.85–110). We can see the story behind this. The shroud is a device to put off a decision as long as possible, and as such Penelope reports it to the unrecognized Odysseus (19.136ff.). The theme is not in itself very conclusive, and the discovery of Penelope's trickery by the Suitors does not force the issue of her marriage as we might expect. There was moreover a different version, which appears when the ghost of Amphimedon says that when Penelope finished the shroud, "in that hour an evil spirit brought Odysseus from somewhere to the border of the land" (24.146–50). This comes from the suspicious conclusion of the *Odyssey*, but its author uses good and independent material; for this is just what the trick of the shroud should have done. Homer must have known it and rejected it for his own less emphatic version because he did not wish Penelope's marriage to be confused with the return of Odysseus, and because he wished this return to be both prolonged and secret.

Another slightly inconclusive theme is that of the seer Theoclymenus. When Telemachus is about to sail from Pylos, Theoclymenus suddenly appears and asks for protection, since he is guilty of murder. Telemachus takes him on board (15.256–81). On arriving in Ithaca Theoclymenus asks where he is to stay, and Telemachus, rather strangely, says with Eurymachus, who is one of the Suitors and a prominent enemy. This conveys the depressed and defeated mood of Telemachus. At this point a hawk flies overhead carrying a dove, and Theoclymenus interprets this as an omen of success, with the result that Telemachus changes his mind and gives other orders for the reception of Theoclymenus (15.525ff.). Later, at the palace, Theoclymenus meets Penelope and tells her with full assurance that Odysseus is already in his own country and plotting evil for the Suitors (17.152–61). As a seer he knows this from the omen of the hawk and the dove. Finally, when the doom of the Suitors is near and one of them has just thrown an ox's foot at Odysseus, they are seized with a frenzy of madness, and Theoclymenus in ringing tones foresees their doom (20.345–57). It is an apocalyptic moment, but it is the last for Theoclymenus. He has done his task, which is to forecast events by augury and vision, but we suspect that in some other version he must have done more, that he may have played a more prominent part in letting Penelope know of her husband's presence or in driving the Suitors to their destruction. The element of the supernatural which he represents adds something to the story but is not fully exploited.

In these loose ends and imperfectly exploited themes we can see traces of the different variants which Homer must have known and from which he had to make his selection. But this is not the problem with the end of the *Odyssey* from 23.297 to 24.548. Here there are indeed unexpected contradictions, and there is perhaps an explanation of them. The two great Alexandrian scholars, Aristarchus and Aristophanes, regarded 23.296, "Then they came gladly to the place of their old bed," as the "end" or the "limit" of the *Odyssey.* We do not know why they thought this. They may conceivably have had external evidence that some good manuscripts ended at this point, or they may have made their decision on the strength of anomalies of language and narrative after this point. We cannot dismiss their view, nor can we deny that in some ways the "continuation" differs in some ways from the rest of the poem, not merely in linguistic solecisms but in actual episodes, like Penelope's web. It is unlikely that the main poet of the *Odyssey* composed this part, but that does not deprive it of all significance. At least it shows how the Homeric manner persisted with adaptations, and how someone felt that the end of the *Odyssey* called for some sort of epilogue.

The *Odyssey* might, in our view, have had a perfectly satisfactory end when Odysseus and Penelope go to bed at 23.296. But someone must have felt that more should be said, and we may ask what advantages, if any, were gained by adding the last passages. Odysseus gives Penelope an account of his adventures, tactfully omitting his infidelities. The audience hardly needs this, and we could assume that Penelope will get the story sooner or later. The appearance of the Suitors in Hades indicates their inferiority to the men of Troy, but not much is made of this, and what is stressed is the comparison between Clytaemnestra and Penelope, which the audience might make for itself. On the other hand the recognition of Odysseus by Laertes has a quiet charm and shows Odysseus in a playful, teasing mood. It is family poetry, and there is something to be said for making Odysseus meet his father after he has met his son and his wife. Moreover the fight between the supporters of Odysseus and the kinsmen of the Suitors indicates that the slaying was not as final as it seemed, and it may have provided a start for new adventures in which

Odysseus leaves Ithaca, as he seems to have done in the *Telegony*. The continuation serves no clear single purpose, but suggests a poet who would like to prolong the story in various ways for different reasons. He may have used old material, at least in Penelope's web, and he has a gift for quiet narrative in the scene with Laertes. Otherwise we miss the swing and the strength of the main poem.

The sources of the *Odyssey* are different from those of the *Iliad* and the difference explains some of its character. If it deals with marvels and monsters, so to a smaller extent does the *Iliad*. In both poems gods interfere with the course of nature. When Aphrodite spirits Paris away from the battlefield (*Iliad*, 3.380) or protects Aeneas (*Iliad*, 5.315–17), it is not very different from when Athene covers Odysseus with a mist in Phaeacia (7.15) or changes his appearance to prevent him being recognized (13.430–33). Though the *Iliad* contains the remarkable scene when the horse of Achilles speaks to him, it is because Hera has for this one occasion given it a human voice (*Iliad*, 19.407ff.), and this is well within the power of the gods. The *Odyssey* differs when its marvels are not caused by the gods but belong to the world of legend. The wind bag of Aeolus, the transformations of Circe, the summoning of ghosts at the end of the world, the monstrosity of Scylla are outside human experience and do not belong to the strictly heroic world of the *Iliad*. In face of them Odysseus conducts himself heroically, as when he insists on hearing the Sirens' song but forestalls disaster by getting himself lashed to the mast (12.178–79). But the monsters which he has to face are outside both human and heroic experience.

Homer evidently saw this and tried to bring his monsters as near as possible to humanity, to relate them to it, and even in some degree to humanize them. This is certainly the case with the Cyclops, who despite his single eye, his bulk "like a wooded peak of tall mountains" (9.190–92), and his cannibalistic gluttony, is made real by his pastoral life, by his care for his flocks, by his affection for his ram. He is hideous and horrible, but not outside comprehension. Comparable in some respects to him is the queen of the Laestrygonians. She lives in a rocky fjord, and all looks easy until the scouts of Odysseus entering her palace, "saw a woman as big as a mountain-peak, and they hated her" (10.113). She grabs one of them and plans to make her supper of him. She is of the same loathsome breed as the Cyclops, but since he has recently received full treatment, she is deftly conveyed in a short sketch. The Sirens, despite their gift of song which lures men to death and the bones of decaying bodies round them (12.45–46), are careful to do no more than invite

Odysseus to listen to them on the latest subjects of song (12.184–92). The exception to this realism is Scylla, who is a monster among monsters, aptly and fully described, with her twelve feet, her six necks, each with a head and three rows of teeth (12.89–91); she seizes six men from the ship of Odysseus and eats them while they are still crying for help and stretching out their hands, so that Odysseus comments:

> "That was the most piteous thing that I saw with my eyes of
> all that I suffered searching out the ways of the sea."
>
> (12.258–59)

Scylla must be descended from tales of sea monsters, of giant krakens and man-slaying cuttlefish, and perhaps because she has some basis in fact Homer feels that he must describe her exactly. She is far from ordinary, and yet one small touch brings her into the compass of living things—her voice is like that of a puppy (12.86). It is quite unexpected and almost absurd, and it is just this that brings it home. The monsters of the *Odyssey* are clearly visualized. Their horror comes not from vagueness but from clearly imagined actions and the menace of a horrible death which they offer. The only approximation to them in the *Iliad* is the Chimaera:

> It was a divine creature, not of human race, in front a lion, in
> the rear a snake, and in the middle a goat, and it breathed the
> terrible strength of flaming fire.
>
> (*Iliad*, 6.180–82)

Description is reduced to the barest essentials, but the Chimaera emerges clearly. This is the Homeric way of looking at monsters, and it is fully developed in the *Odyssey*. It is quite different from the shapeless horrors which the long northern night gives to its dragons.

This controlling realism informs most parts of the *Odyssey* and gives much of its special flavour. It accounts for a certain quiet poetry which is not very noticeable in the *Iliad,* but makes the *Odyssey* friendly and familiar. It finds poetry in quite unassuming and humble subjects, as when Telemachus goes to bed and Euryclea folds his clothes and hangs them on a peg (1.439–40), or his ship sets out in the evening and the wind fills the sail and the dark waves resound about the stern (2.427–29). Life in the palace, despite the disruption caused by the Suitors, follows a routine, and there is a quiet dignity in the reception of guests, the laying out of tables, the scrubbing of them with sponges. In making his raft Odysseus shows a high technical accomplishment, and the mere making has its own interest. It was this that Racine admired so greatly, when he compared its language with Latin:

> Calypso lui donne encore un vilebrequin et des clous, tant Homère est exact à décrire les moindres particularités, ce qui a bonne grace dans le grec, au lieu que le latin est beaucoup plus réservé, et ne s'amuse pas à de si petites choses.
>
> (*Oeuvres complètes*)

Yet, though the Homeric language can say anything that it likes and not lose its force, that is because the poetical vision for which it works is so direct and straightforward. It finds interest and charm everywhere, and is happy to say so.

The same kind of realism can be seen in the characters. We have marked how Odysseus is developed from his old self in the *Iliad,* but he is the only character of any complexity, and that is because legend insisted upon a more than common personality. The others go their own way, and make their individual mark. At the start Telemachus is only a boy, and conscious of it. But he wishes to assert himself, even though he lacks the authority and the experience to do so. His voyage to Pylos makes a man of him. On it he settles his own decisions, and, when he comes back to Ithaca, he is ready for action, and follows and helps his father. Penelope presents rather a special problem. Legend marked her as prudent, and she has kept the Suitors off for ten years, not merely by the stratagem of the web but by other postponements and evasions. Despite long hours of tearful lamentation for her lost husband she keeps her courage, and her sudden appearances among the Suitors reduce them to momentary acquiescence, which cannot all be ascribed to good manners. Her prudence makes her suspicious, and that is why she is so slow to recognize Odysseus as her husband. She and Telemachus are supported by the swineherd Eumaeus and the old nurse Euryclea, and though the first claim of these is their unswerving loyalty to their master, they display an innate nobility in their response to the demands made of them. The party of Odysseus on Ithaca is homogeneous in that it is held together by loyalty to him and hatred of the Suitors. It contains no very powerful personality except the great man himself, but its members are sufficiently distinctive to set him in a full perspective.

The Suitors are beyond dispute deplorable, not in the plebeian way of Thersites but as a degenerate corruption of heroes. They have a high opinion of themselves and no scruples about getting what they want. Antinous differs from Eurymachus only in being more outspokenly brutal. The others conform to type, except perhaps Amphinomus, who has some relics of decency but does not escape death because of them (22.89–94). Their deaths are deserved, as are those of the household of Odysseus who follow them. The beggar Irus, the goatherd Melanthius, the serving-woman Melantho, begin by insulting the unrecognized Odysseus and come to suitable ends. In the Suitors it is hard not to see an embodiment of a heroic society in decay. This is the generation that did not fight at Troy, and their lack of heroic qualities fits the relatively unheroic temper of the *Odyssey.* It makes little attempt to maintain the lofty level of the *Iliad,* and the hero who holds it together is never matched by anyone of his own calibre. Even Alcinous, despite his wealth and kingly conde-scension, is not heroic, and some of his court, notably Laodamas and Euryalus, lack proper courtesy (8.132ff.). This lower tone comes partly from the material of the *Odyssey,* which is concerned not with heroic prowess in war but with wild adventures and a cunning vengeance. It is significant that, when Odysseus kills the Suitors, he has every advantage over them, and though this is due to his foresight, it is not the way in which Achilles would take on an enemy.

In the *Iliad* the intermittent interventions of the gods and the frivolity of some of their actions provide a contrast to the dangers and destruc-tiveness of heroic life; in the *Odyssey* such a contrast is not needed, and the gods are treated with a different intention. The nearest approximation to the spirit of the Deception of Zeus is the song of Demodocus about Ares and Aphrodite (8.266–366), but its purpose is to provide relief before Odysseus starts on the tale of his adventures, and incidentally to throw light on the Phaeacians, who, having no heroic obligations or challenges, are well served by this kind of song. Otherwise the *Odyssey* treats the gods less freely than the *Iliad* and in a more calculated way. They are concerned with human actions, and the council on Olympus, which decides to do something about Odysseus, keeps an eye on such wrongdoing as the behaviour of Aegisthus (1.32–41). Poseidon is entirely justified in maintaining his wrath against Odysseus for blinding Poly-phemus (1.20–21), which leads to his being wrecked on his raft, and incidentally to the ship of the Phaeacians, which takes him to Ithaca, being turned to stone (13.163–64). But apart from these special cases, the dominating part played by the gods in the *Odyssey* is the friendship between Athene and Odysseus. This recalls such occasions in the *Iliad* as when, in the panic after Agamemnon's false proposal to withdraw from Troy, Athene sets Odysseus to restore order (*Iliad,* 2.173–82) or on night operations keeps an eye on him (*Iliad,* 10.245, 277, 482, 497). In the *Odyssey* she is seldom far away. Both on Phaeacia and in Ithaca she is a constant helper and gives Odysseus advice and practical assistance, while in the intervals she instils confidence into his son. She even takes part in the slaughter of the Suitors by deflecting weapons aimed at Odysseus (22.256, 273) and frightening the Suitors by flashing her aegis from the roof (22.297–98). Her character as a virgin-goddess makes it impossible for her to be in love with Odysseus but she holds him in great affection and admiration. They treat each other on equal terms, as when she praises him for his cunning (13.291ff.), or he recalls her kindness to him at Troy (13.314). The Homeric poems have no parallel to so close a companionship between a goddess and a mortal, and though later Greek literature occasionally allows such friendships, it makes much less of them than Homer does of this. It enhances the position of Odysseus as a heroic survivor in an unheroic world. A man of this quality deserves the affection and the support of the gods.

In general the *Odyssey* lacks the sustained splendour of the *Iliad,* has fewer overwhelming moments and a less demanding conception of human worth. The slaughter of the Suitors provides a thrilling climax but lacks the profound pathos of the death of Hector, while the cold, vengeful anger of Odysseus is not comparable to the fiery, devouring passion of Achilles. All is set in a lower key, and this may be due to the nature of the subject and the traditional treatment of it. Folktales and fairy tales, even tales of injured wives and revengeful husbands, need not summon the same powers as the wounded pride of Achilles or the fate of Troy. The *Odyssey* has moments of breathless excitement and moving pathos, but its normal level is less stirring and closer to ordinary experience. Even if tradition was partly responsible for setting this tone, there may be an additional reason for it in the poet's desire to compose a poem nearer to the life that he knew and to the events of every day. By combining these with impossible adventures and enthralling marvels he could set them in a new and brighter light. Longinus thinks that this difference between the *Iliad* and the *Odyssey* is due to the poet's advancing years, and he makes a good observation when he says:

> Accordingly, in the *Odyssey* Homer may be compared to the setting sun, whose greatness remains without its intensity. He does not here maintain so high a level as in those poems of Ilium. His sublimities are not even sustained and free from sinking; there is not the same profusion of passions one after

another, nor the supple and public style, packed with inventions drawn from real life.

(On the Sublime, 9.13)

Longinus assumes that both poems were composed by the same author, and that is something we shall discuss [elsewhere]. For the moment it is enough to assume that they have marked differences, but these can conceivably be ascribed either to a difference of kind established by tradition or to the difference of outlook and temper which a single poet may develop with the advance of years.

The Power of the Word

Norman Austin

The events at the courts are almost all words and thoughts. In the *Odyssey* as a whole, but particularly in the court scenes, conversation is the action. There is a yawning chasm in critical discussion of the *Odyssey* caused by the simple failure to recognize that the *Odyssey* is a poem about words, about the use of language. There is a confusion in criticism between the poem itself and the saga that provides the poem with its external events. What purports to be literary analysis of the poem turns out on inspection to be, often, a discussion as to whether one version of the saga or an event in the saga is early or late, good or bad. While we indulge ourselves in the quest for the original, and perfect, saga, the poem passes us by.

Insofar as the *Odyssey* is related to saga, it is a poem about attitudes towards a saga. It is the account of persons whose lives are shaped by a saga and who in their turn shape it for succeeding generations. From the poem itself we have a clear enough statement on the impossibility of knowing the original saga. The tradition, as the poem depicts it, is totally an oral one. The saga comes to us only in fragments, large and small. Some fragments come from singers who have received the tale from others, others come from the participants in the events; a large fragment comes from the protagonist himself. All these are deposited into the reservoir of oral tradition, and from that reservoir Homer himself draws a piece here, a piece there, to collage them into his poem on the human mind.

When Odysseus first meets Nausikaa he wishes for her "a husband,

From *Archery at the Dark of the Moon.* © 1975 by the Regents of the University of California. University of California Press, 1975.

a home, and like-mindedness [*homophrosyne*], for nothing is stronger," he says, "than when a man and a woman hold a house, both thinking alike in their thoughts [*homophroneonte noemasin*]" (6.181–84). The ideal of harmony between two persons is the keystone of the poem, the *telos* to which it moves. The main action is the process by which Odysseus and Penelope recover their spiritual and psychological harmony. The important scene of the poem is thus the conversation between Odysseus and Penelope in book 19. So pivotal is the scene that it generates a family of allomorphs. A queen's entertainment of a stranger becomes the *topos* of the poem. The queen's hospitality towards the vagrant in Ithaka sets a pattern which another queen will rehearse before her in Scheria, and yet another queen will rehearse with the stranger's son in Sparta. In each of these three instances an anonymous traveller arrives at the queen's court. The community receives him and interrogates him. He conceals his identity at first but slowly becomes integrated into the life of the community. When his integration is sufficiently complete he reveals his identity and his mission. In each case the traveller learns to adapt himself to a variety of persons in the community, but the figure on whose goodwill he most depends is the queen.

These three scenes, around which grow the three acts of the poem, we can for convenience label as follows:

1. Helen's entertainment of Telemachos in Sparta
2. Arete's entertainment of Odysseus in Scheria
3. Penelope's entertainment of Odysseus in Ithaka

By analyzing the dynamics of these scenes, and the correspondences between them, we can learn what Homer has to say about mind discovering its own rhythms and about the harmony it creates with the rhythms of other minds. [Analyses of only the first two of these scenes are included here.]

HELEN AND TELEMACHOS

Telemachos's journey has a thoroughly practical purpose. He is to ascertain information on his father's whereabouts which will govern his future decisions at home. Factual information, however, comprises but half his mission, if as much as that. At a deeper level Telemachos's journey is his education. He must become the young hero capable of sustaining a hero's role in Ithaka, and for that it is necessary for him to be initiated into the heroic world represented by Nestor and Menelaos. But his education requires more than simple exposure to heroic culture. Telemachos must be educated to become the son of Odysseus. The son, in order to become spiritually like the father, traces out a reduced, and to some degree symbolic, journey in imitation of his father. Telemachos duplicates in important ways the kinds of experience Odysseus undergoes. He too must brave the sea to visit unknown peoples; he too will see cities and come to know mind. There will be a powerful king and queen to receive him, as there will be for Odysseus. Like the father, the son will arrive incognito at a magnificent palace, his identity will be recognized, and he will prevail through his charm and find there what he needs for his return. The Telemachy is, as my friend Julie Lamont first pointed out to me, a brilliant example of sympathetic magic. The son imitates the father in a literal fashion first in order to become the father, but the sympathetic action goes further than that. Telemachos also imitates his father in order to secure his father's return. He completes a journey abroad as a magical spell that will ensure that his father too will complete his journey.

The parallels between the two journeys, that of the father and that of the son, are numerous, as we should expect in a poem that understands education as imitation. So numerous, indeed, and so varied, ranging from large thematic structures to minute correspondences in verbal patterns and physical gestures, that mathematical probability should argue against a *Bearbeiter*'s later interference. If the Telemachy is credited to a *Bearbeiter* who has stitched together such an organic prelude from fragments appropriated from the *Odyssey*-poet's oeuvre, we can only praise the Lord that Homer left his papers in such competent hands.

Among the more obvious parallels we note that both father and son must consult a person who is *pepnumenos,* someone with his wits intact. Athena urges Telemachos to address himself first to Nestor, since he is a pepnumenos and will not lie (3.20), and then Nestor advises Telemachos to consult Menelaos since he too is pepnumenos and will not lie (3.323–28). Kirke sends Odysseus to Hades's realm to consult Teiresias, the only person in the underworld whose mind remains pepnumenos (10.494–95). Another parallel is that a substantial part of both journeys is given over to tales of the returns, the *nostoi,* though Telemachos is the initiate who hears them from his hosts and Odysseus is the initiated who narrates them to his hosts. Both father and son find themselves in similar predicaments from which they must extricate themselves gracefully. Both, that is, are entertained royally and are importuned to extend their stay in a rich but alien palace, but must reject the invitations in order to return to a lady whom they have left unprotected at home. Both make the final stage of their return journey accompanied by persons of magical powers: Telemachos sails from Pylos to Ithaka accompanied by Theoklymenos, a distant relative of his Pylian host and a seer with extraordinary mantic powers, and Odysseus is conveyed home by his Phaiakian hosts who have extraordinary navigational powers. Both father and son must look to an imposing king and queen to achieve their objectives, Telemachos to Menelaos and Helen, Odysseus to Alkinoos and Arete.

One parallel is a stellar example of Homer's love of balance and rapport in even the smallest gesture, and an illustration of the psychological essence the poet can concentrate into a gesture. In Sparta, Telemachos is recognized when Menelaos's references to Odysseus, whom he presumes dead, have prompted Telemachos to tears (4.115–16): "Telemachos drew his porphyrian cloak before his eyes. Menelaos recognized him." Helen, entering the hall at that moment, remarks (ll. 141ff.): "I say that I have not seen either man or woman more like the son of great-hearted Odysseus, I mean Telemachos, the baby whom that man left at home when the Achaians went beneath Troy for me, bitch-faced, and they pressed ferocious war." To which Menelaos replies, of the young man hiding his features behind his cloak (ll. 148ff.): "I too am just conceiving that same likeness which you notice. There are Odysseus's feet, these his hands, the glance of his eyes, his head, and his hair above. And here I was just remembering Odysseus in my conversation." Potent indeed is conversation, in which a reference to the person of Odysseus can summon forth his personification.

Odysseus is recognized in a parallel as exact as his differing situation permits. At the Phaiakian court someone has been remembering Odysseus in story, namely Demodokos. Demodokos's remembrance has taken the form of the story of the Wooden Horse, which the visitor to the court had requested, just as the young visitor in Sparta utters a remark that prompts Menelaos's reflections on Odysseus. As Demodokos sings Odysseus bursts into nothing short of a funeral wail, as if (so goes the simile at this point) he were a widow mourning her husband killed before the city walls while protecting his city, his people, and his family (8.532ff.): "He escaped notice of all others but king Alkinoos, who alone remarked him and *recognized* him, as he sat beside him groaning copiously." Whereupon Alkinoos, rather than display bad manners by revealing the name of the stranger in his palace, calls Demodokos to put aside the sweet *phorminx* since the tale he sings is not a *charis* to everyone (ll. 539ff.): "From the moment when the divine singer took up the song our guest has not ceased from shrill lament. A great grief indeed has surrounded him." If Demodokos's charis at this point must be to forgo his song, then Odysseus too must grant a charis in turn, says Alkinoos (ll. 542ff.), for by the mutual exchange of charis everyone, guest and host alike, will enjoy himself, and that would be much better. The charis Alkinoos requests from Odysseus is to restrain his tears and to reveal himself, to reveal, that is, his connection with the subject of Demodokos's song. Alkinoos asks that Odysseus should spell Demodokos awhile and continue the tale from the participant's point of view. Odysseus then reveals the name of the man who, on the occasion of Demodokos's earlier song, had "with stout hands drawn his great porphyrian cloak and shielded his head, and hidden his handsome features" (see 8.84–85). Odysseus then tells/sings a song such as the Phaiakians had never heard, and Alkinoos understands why this man can never stay to become his son-in-law.

Amid the prodigal correlations between the journeys of parent and child, the one most apposite here is that both journeys show a distinct progression in complexity of physical and social structures. Telemachos and Odysseus both move from fairly elementary social milieus to highly organized and sophisticated ones, the progression visible not simply in the external arrangements of life in each culture, but also (and most important) in the psychological subtleties in the characters' speeches. Both father and son move from a situation (or situations, in Odysseus's case) that requires elementary responses to one that demands the highest concentration of finesse and discretion of which they are capable.

Telemachos has only two sites to visit; his journey has, therefore, a simplicity that perhaps makes the structure clearer and prepares us for the more complex pattern in Odysseus's journey. Telemachos's hosts at Pylos and Sparta belong to the heroic world; both Nestor and Menelaos participated in the Trojan War, both have stories to tell of Odysseus. Despite the obvious similarities, a wide contrast is drawn between the two sites, as if they were two opposing poles. Life at Pylos is curiously rustic. Though Nestor has a palace and what seems like unlimited wealth, we hear and see almost nothing of the palace, or of the life lived therein. All the events in the Pylos episode occur outside, on the shore or in the meadow. Similarly, description of social organization is minimal. We know that Nestor has a large household; we see his son Peisistratos play a minor role beside his father, and in the preparations for the great sacrifice to Athena we see something of the community life. All the same, life in Pylos seems strangely solitary and isolated.

In Pylos Telemachos meets a man who can teach him the right

attitudes towards gods and men. Nestor is courteous, hospitable, cooperative, not to mention being a good raconteur. He strikes us, however,
as a person of limited perception. He entertains unaware a goddess and
the son of the man whom he calls his most trusted counselor. He recognizes Athena only after she has assumed her bird shape and flown
away. He comments on the similarity in speech between Telemachos and
his father (another reminder that words are action in the poem), but this
only after Telemachos has already revealed his identity. Nestor can tell
Telemachos nothing of Odysseus's whereabouts; the best he can suggest
is that Telemachos visit Menelaos. Nestor's role seems to be a preparatory
one, as is Nausikaa's role in the Scherian act, or Eumaios's role in the
Ithakan act. Nestor points Telemachos in the direction of a more important scene.

The scene in Pylos is important as Telemachos's introduction to the
civilized life that has been lacking for many years in Ithaka. The episode,
however, remains straightforward and relatively unsophisticated. The
contrast between Pylos and Sparta is remarkable. At Sparta, Telemachos
is thrust into a more urbane society of a greater complexity and intelligence, where the demands on him are proportionately higher. No longer
the rustic feudalism of Pylos. Now the setting is a palace, and the palace
itself becomes a significant part of his experience. Telemachos was
slightly bashful when first approaching Nestor, but timidity becomes
utter astonishment when he views Menelaos's palace. It is so far outside
the range of his experience that he is led to compare it with Zeus's palace
on Olympos. The communal life in the palace is as elaborate and impressive as the architecture. The whole palace is a hive of activity; a
wedding feast is in progress when Telemachos arrives, with a singer,
dancers, and acrobats providing entertainment. The magnificence of the
palace, of the feast and its entertainment, the abundance of precious objects in the palace (Telemachos receives no guest-gift from Nestor, but
only the loan of a chariot), and the presence of two powerful and equal
rulers (rather than a single one as at Pylos) all conspire to suggest technological and political achievements far in advance of those found on the
sandy shore of Pylos.

There is, as we have now come to predict, a correlation between
technological achievement and mental acumen. Menelaos and Helen ex-
ceed Nestor in sophistication as much as their palace exceeds his in splen-
dor. Menelaos is sufficiently alert to overhear Telemachos's comparison,
made sotto voce to Peisistratos, of Menelaos's palace with Olympian
architecture. At Pylos, by contrast, Athena prays, aloud presumably, to

Poseidon to grant "Telemachos and me success," but Nestor is apparently distracted since he must ask the strangers' identity immediately thereafter (3.60ff.). We do not customarily place Menelaos among the shrewdest of Homeric heroes, yet in the *Odyssey* he is quick enough to recognize Telemachos without prior knowledge; his discretion leads him to debate whether he should reveal his awareness to Telemachos (4.116–19). Menelaos demonstrates his discretion further the next day when he searches out Telemachos and asks him, in private conference, the real reason for his visit.

Helen is drawn as a person even more perceptive than her husband. She too recognizes their young guest, and her recognition is instantaneous and sure, whereas Menelaos gives the impression of some vacillation. Though Helen had never seen the baby born to Odysseus, she recognizes in the person before her the exact image of Odysseus as he was when he went to Troy twenty years before (4.141–46). At a later point in the first evening she demonstrates her graciousness by supplying the drug *nepenthes,* and she herself becomes Nepenthes who turns remembrance from sorrow to joy by relating old tales of Odysseus's stratagems. When it is time for Telemachos's departure from Sparta, it is Helen who is quick to interpret the bird omen as propitious for Telemachos and his family. Odysseus is warned that his passage home from Scheria depends specifically on Arete's approval. There is no formal statement to credit Helen with such preeminent authority in the Telemachy. Her role, however, is certainly the dominant one. She recognizes Telemachos before he identifies himself; she has the ability to turn the evening's lamentation into good cheer; she can interpret an omen favorably for Telemachos. In such acts, indicative of her dominance, we see the evidence of Penelope's influence extending even to the structure of the Telemachy.

The poem's first exemplars of family homophrosyne are the king and queen of Sparta. As hosts they are impeccable—solicitous and discreet. But more remarkable is their unanimity. They have the same thought, as we have seen, on the identity of their still anonymous visitor. They have the same thoughts when it comes time to change the lugubrious mood of Telemachos's first evening at their court. To change the mood, each tells a story about Troy, and in their stories they show themselves as perfect complements for each other.

The stories they tell have to do with Odysseus's cleverness, and both are of the Greek penetration into the city of Troy. Nestor had talked of Odysseus as the most gifted of orators. Menelaos and Helen now give paradigms of Odysseus as the most gifted at inventing and executing schemes. Menelaos tells the story of the Wooden Horse that Odysseus had devised. Helen tells of Odysseus's spying mission, when he had entered Troy disguised as a beggar. In giving their fragments of the Odysseus saga they fulfill their social obligations towards their tearful young guest. At the same time, however, they use the stories as the medium through which to speak to, and about, each other. An important element in Menelaos's tale is Helen's counterstratagem for testing the Wooden Horse, a stratagem that would have doomed the Greeks had it not been for Odysseus's ability to control even that emergency. What emerges from his story is that Helen too is a person of clever strategies, the only peer, in fact, of Odysseus. Helen's tale is also of strategy and counterstrategy, and again the principals are Odysseus and Helen. In her story, Odysseus planned another strategy for gaining entrance into Troy, but once again she was capable of penetrating the disguise. Her story is as much self-flattery as it is flattery of Odysseus. She takes pains, however, to give Menelaos his due. She compliments him by claiming that her desire was to leave Troy and to return to him. Her interception of Odysseus was prompted, so we are to understand from her version of the tale, by her desire to be reunited with her husband. Whether true or not, it is at least a nice reflection on the marital homophrosyne that figures so large in this poem.

With what delicacy those two masters of tact touch on the catastrophe of which they were the joint sponsors. Even while admitting their responsibility, how deftly they can temper it so as to caress each other's sensibilities, Helen by acknowledging Menelaos the equal of any man in both looks and intelligence (cf. 4.264), Menelaos by acknowledging Helen as the only peer of Odysseus, and by crediting her with the gift of impersonating every man's wife—an admission that seems to mitigate, to a degree, Paris's mistake in abducting her.

Menelaos and Helen are ideal hosts in all practical ways, but hospitality in the *Odyssey* includes more than keeping conversation and wine flowing. It requires an intuitive understanding of the hidden meaning behind spoken words, an understanding even of unspoken thoughts. Homer has endowed Menelaos, and more especially Helen, with such gifts in ample measure. It is interesting to see Telemachos responding in reciprocal fashion to their hospitality. He becomes more adept in social forms. When Menelaos presses him to stay and promises prize horses and a chariot as his guest-gift, Telemachos replies in such a way as to elicit Menelaos's highest admiration. Telemachos declines the offer by appealing to the fictitious impatience of his friends waiting in Pylos, but at the same time he compliments Menelaos and depreciates himself and his little island home. With good reason Menelaos has to laugh, grasp Telemachos by the hand, and exclaim: "You are of good blood, my son, by what you say" (4.609ff.). A second time, at the end of Telemachos's stay in Sparta, Menelaos presses him to tarry longer and offers him a tour through the mainland, but Telemachos declines, again with a white lie, though this lie is a refined shadow of the truth. Telemachos pleads his fear that in his own and his father's absence from Ithaka he may lose some precious object from his halls (15.90–91). His meaning could not be clearer, even though propriety forbids him from putting his real meaning into words. Nor could Odysseus himself have framed his anxiety in so delicate a manner. The straightforward but bashful young man of book 1 has achieved, by the time he leaves Sparta, an elegant self-possession.

Telemachos will give ample proof in Ithaka that his physical journey abroad has increased his mental powers. Just how great the increase will be we can deduce from his behavior when he decides on the disposition of the seer Theoklymenos to whom he had given asylum on his ship. On the shore at Ithaka, Telemachos first suggests that Theoklymenos stay with his archenemy Eurymachos, Penelope's most aggressive suitor. In Sparta, as we have seen, Telemachos is quite capable of bending the truth if discretion so demands. Here we find him saying the outright opposite of his truth. He praises Eurymachos as the best possible host, but the extravagance of the young orator's encomium betrays his sarcasm. If Telemachos can call Eurymachos the bright son of a dazzling father, a man whom the folk in Ithaka behold as a god (15.519–20), that can scarcely be Telemachos's personal persuasion. Athena had already warned Telemachos at Sparta that Eurymachos was the man most likely to win his mother and carry off his possessions in Telemachos's absence (15.17–19). Zeus well understands the irony in the young orator's words, even if modern scholars do not. Zeus sends his omen, which Theoklymenos turns to Telemachos's favor, his interpretation being an assurance that Eurymachos has not won yet and Telemachos is still master of his house (see 15.531–34). Telemachos then reverses himself and entrusts this wise seer, who has just proved his worth, to his loyal friend Peiraios, whom we expected him to nominate as Theoklymenos's host in the first place. Quick thinking for the young fellow who was once too shy to address

Nestor without Athena's encouragement, now to test his fate and his newfound seer in a single deft operation. His camouflage of his motives is worthy of the man whom he had gone forth to imitate.

Arete and Odysseus

Leaving Telemachos on the shore at Ithaka to practice there the disguises his travels have taught him, we can turn to observe the father now imitating the son. In Odysseus's journey we see even more clearly the correlation between mental perception and the degree and kind of organization. Odysseus moves from dealing with such obtuse figures as Polyphemos at one pole to the masters of nuance at Scheria at the other pole. It requires little intelligence to outwit Polyphemos; Odysseus needs only minimal cunning, and a grain or two of prudence, to gain the advantage over brutish strength. All it takes, really, is a pun. A single word lays the giant low, if it be the right word. Kirke, almost as savage as Polyphemos, needs a more sophisticated response. Hermes must supply Odysseus with a magical drug and certain rites that will outspell Kirke's spell by a kind of homeopathic magic. Once subdued, she and Odysseus meet as equals—no, never quite as equals, since human compassion is alien to her nature. She must be reminded that Odysseus cannot enjoy her hospitality while his men remain bewitched. When Odysseus wishes to take his leave she sends him down to the underworld, and only after his return thence does she offer help for his journey. The sinister always adheres to her nature, however correctly she plays the hostess for Odysseus.

In Kalypso the sinister has been submerged entirely. Whatever noxious influences may radiate from her name, her location, her ancestry or her superhuman nature are kept under control, though when she grants Odysseus his departure he shudders in fear that she might unloose those influences on him. Instead of being the fairy tale witch like Kirke, Kalypso is entirely humanized, a full person rather than a *Märchen-Mädchen*. Her conversation with Hermes is a civilized one, resonant with the nuances between two persons who understand and sympathize with each other. She is angry, but still hospitable. The subject of their colloquy remains anonymous. Hermes is hesitant and apologetic, and with a tactful gesture refrains from naming the man whom Kalypso must release. She replies, also without naming Odysseus. She raises the problem of a ship and crew, but Hermes does not trouble to address himself to an obstacle so obviously factitious. He only repeats that she must obey Zeus if she would avoid his hard anger (5.85–147). That same day, in her last conversation with Odysseus, Kalypso again reveals her elegant style (5.203ff.). She bids Odysseus *chaire* for his voyage home, if home is what he really wants. She warns him of the woes lying in wait for him between her island and Ithaka, woes he could avoid by staying and choosing immortality with Kalypso rather than mortality with Penelope. It is an attempt at seduction, of course, but so phrased as to permit Odysseus to tender his regrets with the least possible embarrassment for both parties.

Odysseus is as tactful in his reply as Kalypso is in her request (ll. 251ff.). He is well aware, he says, that there can be no comparison between Penelope and Kalypso, a nymph who knows not death nor age. Even so, and despite sufferings still in store, his heart is set on his returning home and beholding the day of his homecoming. The clever little Noman has come a long way from Polyphemos's cave. In that encounter a single word was weapon enough. Here too, on Kalypso's island, Odysseus achieves his goal with words, but there is no trickery in them. No longer weapons, words are beginning at last, in this episode, to be the medium for communication between two persons, for hearing the mind of the other and revealing one's own. In the Kyklops episode a word severs, alienates, polarizes. Here words have an integrative function. Even if Odysseus cannot stay with Kalypso, yet in their final conversation they have achieved a psychological harmony that can outspell any physical union. Kalypso prepares Odysseus for his experience in Scheria, where again his only tools will be words. The kind of integration of two opposing wills, which we see informing Odysseus's last conversation with Kalypso, will be repeated, in greater detail and on a larger canvas, in Scheria. The Scheria episode is a large-scale amplification of Odysseus's conversation with Kalypso.

The first soul Odysseus meets in Scheria is Nausikaa, and the first words he utters reveal the gulf now separating us from Kyklopean caves, and even from nymphs' rustic grottoes. Trickery, if trickery is the right word for Odyssean *dolos,* has now been transformed into charm: αὐτίκα μειλίχιον καὶ κερδαλέον φάτο μῦθον (6.148), so Homer describes Odysseus's speech to Nausikaa. It is a speech compounded of honey and profit. He lays a spell on everyone in Scheria, on Nausikaa first, then on Arete and Alkinoos, but there is no magic *moly* this time. He is on his own, master of his own destiny, and the *moly* must emerge from his personality. The Phaiakians, themselves a charmed folk, respond to those who have the gift to charm.

The Phaiakians give every sign of intelligence in the organization of their lives. But their monarchs are especially recognized for their intelligence: Alkinoos "knows thoughts from the gods," which is a Homeric way of talking about extraordinary perception (θεῶν ἄπο μήδεα εἰδώς, 6.12); Arete has a *noos esthlos* (7.73). Their daughter is no less endowed. All three members of the family show their intelligence in their behavior towards each other.

Nausikaa, whom we see first, invents a false pretext when she asks her father for the use of the wagon. Athena had put marriage in her mind during the previous night, but Nausikaa is wise enough to camouflage her true motives. Later, at the river, she shows her poise by standing her ground before the briny apparition who rises from the sea and then by calmly arranging for all his needs. Her full charm emerges only in her conversation with Odysseus when she discusses the best strategy for his entry into the city and palace. She had already exclaimed to her handmaidens, when she had seen Odysseus bathed and clothed (6.243–45): "Now he seems like a god. . . . Would that such a man might be called my husband . . . and it might please him to remain here." But now as she approaches the city with Odysseus, Nausikaa introduces the subject of marriage in a more coquettish manner. Odysseus should enter the city separately, she says, otherwise some fellow of the baser sort, seeing them together, might say (6.276ff.): "Who is this handsome and distinguished stranger with Nausikaa? Her husband he'll be I suppose. . . . Perhaps a god came down in answer to her prayer and he will possess her all her days. Better for her if she finds her husband from elsewhere, since she scorns all her local suitors, and many fine Phaiakians she has as her suitors too."

Modest she is, but modesty doesn't preclude wit. In a brief speech Nausikaa succeeds in relaying much information about herself through the medium of a fictitious gossip. She finds the stranger like a god, so the pretended gossip reveals; she herself has many of the best men in Scheria as her suitors but she has spurned them and prayed to the gods for someone better. And now a better has appeared, like a god. Alas that such winsome oratory is to no avail. The stranger will not tarry and Nausikaa parts from him the next day with the prayer that he may remember her for the guest-gift she had given him, namely his life.

Alkinoos's intelligence shows itself in intuition and discretion. He understands that marriage lies behind Nausikaa's request for the wagon but he keeps his knowledge to himself. He is well aware of what it must mean when his marriage-minded daughter brings a handsome stranger up from the sea, and accordingly he lets the stranger know of his personal feelings (7.312ff.): "Being such as you are, and with your mind thinking as mine does, would that you could have my daughter and be called my son-in-law. . . . But no Phaiakian will hold you here against your will." An honest declaration but without pressure. The way is open for Odysseus to accept or to decline as he chooses.

The next day brings Alkinoos several more occasions to exercise his diplomacy. He schedules athletics in place of song when he sees the melancholy effect of Demodokos's song on the stranger. Here his tact forbids his mentioning the real reason for the change in activity; he merely explains that the court has had its surfeit of food and song and should go outside (8.98ff.). When an incident occurring during the athletic performances almost devolves into a fracas, and Odysseus retaliates to insults by proving himself superior to the Phaiakians at their own sport, Alkinoos diplomatically reestablishes Phaiakian self-esteem by suggesting a change from athletics to dance. Later, when evening comes on and Demodokos takes up another song, Alkinoos again observes the stranger's discomfiture and again calls a halt to the song that is not pleasing to everyone. This time he explains the reason for this intrusion and calls on Odysseus to identify himself. It is the only occasion when Alkinoos resorts to something close to a peremptory command, but he is justified in so doing since he and Arete have already tried several times unsuccessfully to elicit Odysseus's identity. Arete had asked Odysseus point-blank the previous evening but Alkinoos had proceeded more indirectly, hinting once that the stranger might be a god (7.199ff.) and once calling Odysseus "this stranger—I do not know who he is" (8.28). Since Odysseus has resisted all attempts, direct and indirect, Alkinoos must resort to a more insistent tone.

If Alkinoos's insistence is necessary, it also has the beauty of timing. Everything has been prepared for Odysseus's revelation—he has competed with the young men in athletics, he has won the heart of the princess, he has charmed the citizenry into giving generously from their possessions, and his exploits are in the bardic repertory. Alkinoos, in interrupting the story of the Wooden Horse to call for Odysseus's name, makes the best-timed interruption in literature.

Arete too shows the same qualities as her husband and daughter. The best example of her perspicacity occurs in the scene in the palace when all the other guests have been dismissed for the night. Only Alkinoos and Arete are left to question Odysseus in private. When they are alone with Odysseus she slyly reveals, by a casual question on Odysseus's attire, that she is quite as shrewd and discreet as he. She recognizes the clothes on Odysseus "which she herself had made with her womenfolk," and she asks Odysseus (7.237–39): "Who are you? Who gave these clothes to you?" Odysseus in answering her second question conveniently omits to answer her first, an omission that Arete overlooks because Alkinoos interrupts to ventilate his paternal annoyance at Nausikaa's deficient sense of hospitality.

Here is an apparent irregularity: Arete asks a question and is, it seems, indifferent to Odysseus's failure to answer it. An irregularity invariably brings out the analyst in us, to root around for the *Bearbeiter*'s tracks, and sure enough the *Arete-frage,* as German scholarship has named the problem, has had its share of researchers to piece together the theory of multiple authorship which will best explain Arete's silence. The question is misformulated, however, unless the formulation explicitly recognizes the spiritual ambience in Scheria. This is not the giant's cave, where language must be perforce raw and violent. Here language is graceful, its movement an insinuation. Arete is a sensitive interrogator and Odysseus a sensitive respondent. When a mother sees a strange man wearing the very clothes her marriageable daughter took to the river in the morning, her first concern must surely be for her daughter. Arete's question, "Who are you?" is not the regular formula of polite encounter, since on this occasion it really means, "What is your relationship to my daughter?" Arete's concern leaks through the tactful irony of her second question, when she allows Odysseus to know that she has noticed his attire. If a man, attired in someone else's clothes, finds himself face to face with a person who intimates that she is the source of that same attire, such a man, if prudent, will address himself first to explaining how those clothes came into his possession. This is what prudent Odysseus does. Fortunately, his explanation distracts Alkinoos into an excursus on his daughter's manners, and the answer to Arete's first question is conveniently held in abeyance. Odysseus and Arete emerge from their first encounter in a draw. She uses her question to reveal herself as a perceptive woman who will not be easily fooled. He, recognizing a challenge, succeeds in "fooling" her anyway by giving only circumstantial information about himself while still keeping his incognito.

"Nothing is stronger than when, thinking alike in their thoughts, a man and woman hold a house together." Arete and Alkinoos are the poem's second exemplars of that domestic harmony which Odysseus praises as the *summum bonum.* Theirs is a family that thinks in the same way, thinks the same thoughts. Nausikaa need not mention marriage for her father to understand. Arete and Alkinoos see a stranger in their halls dressed in the clothes Nausikaa had taken to the river and they understand what she intended when she gave them to him. Alkinoos sees Odysseus weep, even at the moment when he is concealing his grief, and understands. The family notices details unobserved by others and, whether divulging information or eliciting it, know how to phrase themselves with the right degree of ambiguity so as to conceal as much as they reveal.

Odysseus, to win this family as his allies, must be as adept and perceptive as they; he must become one of them. He must gain their respect by understanding their indirect questions. He must show by *his* style that he recognizes their style. Charis fills the air of Scheria. Nausikaa's handmaidens have their beauty from the *Charites* (6.18); when Odysseus defends himself against Euryalos's insults, Alkinoos finds Odysseus's words οὐκ ἀχάριστα (8.236); Odysseus discourses on charis in his reply to Euryalos's taunts (8.166ff.). Charis is distributed, he says, in varying degrees and kind. One man is a match for the gods in physique but no charis crowns his words (ll. 174–75). Another man is inferior in physique "but god crowns his form with words, and people take pleasure in looking on him. He speaks surely and sweetly and he stands out in the assembly. As he goes through the town they look upon him as a god" (ll. 169–73; cf. Stanford's translation). Charis is the *Odyssey*'s word for style and Odysseus in his speech on the diversity of charis opts plainly for the charis of words as superior to all forms of charites. Words garland a man, says Odysseus, and endow him with a beauty that all admire.

Odysseus proclaims speech as the highest form of charis. From their speeches to each other and to Odysseus we should deduce that Odysseus's view coincides exactly with that of Alkinoos and his family. But even without their speeches we should find evidence of their concurrence in the high stature they accord to Odysseus for his words. Odysseus, naked as a savage, frames a speech in praise of Nausikaa's beauty and Nausikaa's response is to call him "no mean or witless fellow" (οὔτε κακῷ οὔτ' ἄφρονι φωτὶ ἔοικας, 6.187). When Odysseus assures Alkinoos that he is far from being a god, but instead the most wretched of mortals, the assembled guests praise the stranger and bid Alkinoos accede to his request for aid "since he had spoken *kata moiran*" (7.227). When Odysseus defends Nausikaa for her discretion in leaving him to make his way into the palace alone, Alkinoos praises him for his mind. When Odysseus compliments the Phaiakians on their dance, Alkinoos is so pleased at the stranger's showing himself pepnumenos (see 8.388) that he calls for twelve kings to bring gifts from their treasures for the stranger. Earlier, Nausikaa too had called Odysseus a man of understanding, shortly after his first speech to her (οὐκ ἀπίνυσσεω, 6.258). Odysseus's words always prompt a recognition of his intelligence.

Scheria is the showplace of the arts. The Phaiakians are proficient first in manual crafts, in sailing, husbandry, weaving, in the building of artifacts, houses, furniture, and ships. Their arts also include the fine arts—sculpture, ball games for the girls, dancing and athletic contests for the young men. Scheria is the only place within Homeric geography to have a plastic art that frankly imitates for the pleasure of imitation, as witness the mosaic watchdog given to them by Hephaistos and the palace sconces made in the likeness of torchbearers. Everywhere there is craft, and the charis shining from objects which testifies to the craftsmen's success at their creation.

If speech is clearly the highest form of craft in Scheria, and its charis the highest form of charis, within the category of speech there is one form superior to all others which holds in itself the highest concentration of charis. Supreme of the imitative arts is that of the singer. When Odysseus is about to request from Demodokos the song of the Wooden Horse, he sends a gift to the singer and says (8.479–81): "Among all men singers have their share of honor and reverence since the Muse has taught them, and she loves the tribe of bards." He continues by praising Demodokos personally (ll. 487–91): "Far above all mortals I honor you. Either the Muse taught you, or it was Apollo. . . . You sing the tale as if you had been present yourself, or had heard it from someone there." As Odysseus is about to begin his story he leads off with a preamble on the charis of poetry (9.5ff.): "There is no accomplishment with greater charis than the good will (euphrosyne) which possesses everyone within a group, as they sit in order and listen to the singer, while the tables are laden with food and drink, and the wine steward draws wine from the bowl and carries it around."

The banquet and its accompanying song, that is the greatest charis for Odysseus. So it is for the Phaiakians who respond to Odysseus, when he substitutes for Demodokos, as if he were the prince of singers. After Odysseus, in the course of his tale, finishes the catalogue of the famous heroines in the underworld, Arete is moved to remark on the storyteller's physical beauty, mirroring his inner beauty (11.336ff.): "How does this man seem to you in physique, in stature, and in his well-balanced phrenes?" Alkinoos too compliments the substitute poet, and again the emphasis is on both the mind within and the physical appearance without

(11.363ff.): "You are not one of those thievish rogues who fit together lies. On you there is a form from your words [*morphe*; cf. Odysseus himself on the capacity of words to bestow *morphe*, 8.170], and your *phrenes* within are good." Arete calls for those in the hall to reward Odysseus's words with gifts, and Alkinoos repeats her call when Odysseus's tale is done. He asks for gifts from all the assembled company for "it would be hard for a single man to render due charis with his present" (13.15). The wealth Odysseus carries with him from Scheria to his home is not gratuitous; it is earned wealth.

Odysseus's words win him first Nausikaa's trust, then asylum in Alkinoos's court. His tact and diplomacy are rewarded by gifts which pour in to mark his increasing favor on the island. When his words take shape as poetry the king and queen of the society are moved to open admiration, which they demonstrate with yet more gifts and the guarantee of a safe passage home. On Kirke's island Odysseus had recourse to a magical drug to reinforce his power. By the time he reaches Scheria stage props like *moly* disappear. Athena counsels Odysseus that he must win over Arete's mind if he would achieve his homecoming (7.75–76): "For if she think kindly thoughts in her *thymos,* then there is hope to see friends and home again." Now on his own (as is Telemachos in Sparta, without Athena/Mentor's presence to encourage him), Odysseus must learn (or prove) that only mind can captivate mind. At Scheria, magic is an energy that emanates from within—Odysseus learns to replace the charm of drugs with the charm of poetry.

Eyeing the stranger as a prospective son-in-law, Alkinoos addresses him as a person "who thinks the very thoughts I myself think" (7.312). When Odysseus documents, in a variety of ways, that his thought waves are in alignment with those emanating from all the individuals at the Scherian court, then he is ready for the ordeal in Ithaka, where all the lessons learned in prior locations will be put to their severest test.

"Reverse Similes" and Sex Roles in the *Odyssey*

Helene P. Foley

Two surprisingly similar similes mark the first meeting of Penelope and Odysseus and their hard-won reunion. In the first (19.108–14) Odysseus compares the reputation (*kleos*) of Penelope to that of a good and just king whose land and people prosper under him. Penelope replies that the gods destroyed her beauty on the day of Odysseus's departure for Troy; if he were to return, her life and kleos would be fairer and greater. In the second (23.233–40) Odysseus is as welcome to Penelope as land to a shipwrecked sailor worn down by his battle with the surf. This simile at once recalls the situation of Odysseus before he struggles to land on Phaeacia (5.394–98). Thus both similes equate Penelope with a figure like Odysseus himself, as he has been and will be.

These two similes comparing a woman to a man form part of a group of similes of family or social relationship clustering almost exclusively around the incident in Phaeacia and the family of Odysseus as it struggles to recover peace and unity on Ithaca. Many of these similes, like the two mentioned above, also evoke in the comparison an inversion of social role or a social theme with an equivalent difference of focus or point of view. Men are compared to women. In book 8 (523–31) the weeping Odysseus is compared to a woman weeping over the body of her husband lost in war. As she mourns him enemy soldiers strike her shoulders and lead her off to slavery. The conqueror of Troy is identified with the most helpless of his former victims. Fathers are equated with children; Odysseus finds the land of Phaeacia as welcome as the life of a

From *Arethusa* 11, nos. 1–2 (Spring/Fall 1978). © 1978 by the Department of Classics, State University of New York at Buffalo.

father recovered from sickness is to his children (5.394–98). Telemachus in his reunion with the swineherd Eumaeus is greeted as a loving father greets a son returned from ten years of travel; yet it is Odysseus, the real father who is present to observe this embrace, who has returned from travels of considerable length (16.17–20). Telemachus and Odysseus lament at their reunion more intensely than sea-eagles robbed of their unfledged young (16.216–18). Odysseus has just regained his son; yet Homer marks the moment with an image of bereavement, of parents deprived of their young.

These "reverse similes," as I shall call them, seem to suggest both a sense of identity between people in different social and sexual roles and a loss of stability, an inversion of the normal. The comparison of the joy of Penelope to that of a shipwrecked sailor has been interpreted, for example, as Homer's deliberate identification of Odysseus and his like-minded wife, or as one of a series of images of safety from the sea. In this paper, however, I am interested in the larger pattern: why are there so many similes with this consistent change of perspective or reversal of social role in the comparison, and in particular, what is the meaning of the elaborate images of sexual inversion? How do these reverse-sex similes clarify the overall structure and meaning of the relations between man and wife?

The history of festival and comedy provide numerous examples of a world disrupted or inverted, then restored or renewed. Symbolic inversion of the sexes is frequently part of the process. From Aristophanes's Lysistrata to Shakespeare's Rosalind women in literature have assumed men's roles to restore and redefine the institutions of peace—marriage and the family—and to provide an avenue for corrective criticism of the status quo. In festival and comedy the marriage relation, in which the female is subordinate to the male, is used to express, reinforce or criticize a far larger range of hierarchical social and economic relations. In the *Odyssey* direct symbolic inversion of the sexes is delicately reserved for a few prominently placed similes. Yet these similes can be interpreted as a significant part of a larger pattern of social disruption and restoration in the epic. Throughout his journey Odysseus experiences many cultures whose social order is an incomplete or inverted version of his own Ithaca, including variations on the place of women and the limits on their sexual, social and political roles. In a similar way, voluntarily (through disguise) or involuntarily, Odysseus adopts or experiences a wide range of social roles other than his own. Penelope does not take inappropriate advantage of her opportunity to wield power in Odysseus's absence; yet to maintain his kingship she must come close as a woman can to doing so.

Odysseus regains home in the wake of a disruption of normal economic, social and ethical relations on Ithaca. Yet neither the characteristic form of social reproduction on Ithaca, nor its particular hierarchical social and sexual relations are fully resumed until, through the events of the poem, they have been reargued, reclarified and voluntarily reaffirmed by all parties concerned. The continual play with social and sexual categories in the poem results not in social change but in a more flexible interpretation of social roles, and in a new understanding of what form of social and economic relations makes possible the continuity of culture on Ithaca. In the elaborate negotiations leading up to the recognition of Penelope and Odysseus, Homer, like Shakespeare in his middle comedies, manipulates the potential threat of social inversion which underlies the travels and the reverse-sex similes. The power which Penelope has legitimately and skillfully wielded is not transferred by her to Odysseus until she has—albeit unconsciously—regained both his complete trust and power in her own domestic sphere. Homer's extensive treatment of Penelope's role in maintaining the kingship for Odysseus's return, and the length and elaboration of the recognition process between men and women throughout the poem reveal the mutual interdependence of husband and wife in the structure of Homeric society.

The poem begins with a family and society barely maintaining order in the absence of its father and king Odysseus. The Suitors continually waste Odysseus's economic resources in direct violation of the fundamental principles of "Odyssean" society, the mutual obligations of host and guest. The young men of the island insist on wooing a woman of an older generation instead of reproducing their households with women of the appropriate age. The Ithacan assembly has not met in years, and public opinion no longer effectively protects the household of its king. Telemachus, having no room to grow into his patrimony, finds his relations with his mother becoming difficult. Odysseus's mother has died longing for her son; his father still pines for him in lonely squalor.

In this situation Penelope plays a critical role. She alone engages in an active struggle to maintain the cultural norm. She, not Odysseus's *dēmos,* dares to reprove the Suitors' violation of the social order. Despite her difficult situation she periodically attempts to renew Odysseus's wealth by extracting bridal gifts from the Suitors. The Homeric king makes such gift-getting a primary object. She distracts the Suitors from quarreling by exciting their hopes of gaining her hand. The dissolution of such quarrels of the young is a kingly function, as is confirmed by both Alcinous's role in Phaeacia and the simile at 12.439–41, where Odysseus clings to a fig tree over Charybdis until the time when a man leaves the assembly for supper, a man who decides the many quarrels of litigious young men. Penelope receives and cross-examines visitors, and tries to maintain standards of hospitality and a network of communication in Odysseus's disrupted family. She keeps Laertes informed with messages; her deceiving web was an act of familial piety, a shroud for her father-in-law. With the exception of the weaving, these are all social functions which Penelope ultimately transfers to the male members of her family, first to Telemachus, then to Odysseus. At 4.791–93 Penelope is compared to a beleaguered lion. Lion images are typically reserved for heroic men. In the disrupted Ithaca of the early books of the *Odyssey* Penelope, far from being the passive figure of most Homeric criticism, has come remarkably close to enacting the role of a besieged warrior.

Penelope achieves this uneasy victory by a woman's weapons: her Athena-like intelligence, her weaving, and her power to order the household. Circe, Calypso, the Sirens, Helen, and Penelope all have a special power to stop or transcend change in the sphere under their control. In the pursuit of Helen and immortality in war, Helen's former suitors give up ten years of their lives at Troy. The Sirens offer immortal knowledge to those who surround them, but at the sacrifice of natural life. Circe maintains an unchanging existence on her island by transforming her guests from threatening humans to tame animals. At Sparta, Helen relieves her guests from painful memories with a drug which numbs the effects of time. Like Circe, Penelope has turned her guests into swine, into unmanly banqueters, lovers of dance and song rather than war, who are shown, in their failure to string the bow, to be no match for Odysseus. To keep open a place for Odysseus she has symbolically stopped change on Ithaca. All the young men of the kingdom woo Penelope; they are thus prevented from maturing into husbands and warriors, potential rivals to Telemachus or Odysseus. Whatever the true social status of Penelope—and it has aroused much controversy—the poet suggests that she has the power to bring the kingship with her; the Suitors explicitly compete not merely for her beauty but to achieve this political ambition. Similarly, she controls the sexual feelings which might lead her to a new marriage by deliberately maintaining a state of frozen grief. In book 19 Penelope compares herself to the nightingale, daughter of Pandareus, who eternally bewails the loss of her child (ll. 518–23). The image expresses

Penelope's suspension of time on Ithaca, as does another image, continually evoked, of the youthful Odysseus before his departure for Troy. In a comparable position Penelope uses on the men surrounding her the weapons of Helen and Circe not to destroy but to maintain the cultural order. Yet in her effort to preserve Ithaca for Odysseus she cannot stop change entirely; thus the maturing of Telemachus creates increasing tensions for Penelope at the opening of the poem. The unnatural situation on Ithaca comes playfully close to an unintended solution; Telemachus emerges as the only man aside from Odysseus who can win his mother in the contest of the bow.

For all her feminine intelligence in maintaining the material conditions for the survival of Odysseus's household, and thus for his kingship, and even in performing such kingly functions as mediating the quarrels of the restless young, Penelope, because she lacks physical force, can only stop change on Ithaca. She cannot restore it to full social growth. From this perspective we can begin to understand Odysseus's compliment in comparing her fame to that of a just and pious king (19.107–14), following a teasing—or hinting—refusal to discuss his own identity:

> Lady, no mortal man on the endless earth would have cause
> to find fault with you; your fame goes up into the wide
> > heaven,
> as of some king who, as a blameless man and god-fearing,
> and ruling as lord over many powerful people,
> upholds the way of good government, and the black earth
> > yields him
> barley and wheat, his trees are heavy with fruit, his
> > sheepflocks
> continue to bear young, the sea gives him fish, because of
> his good leadership, and his people prosper under him.
> > (Translated by Richmond Lattimore)

These are Odysseus's first words to Penelope. The moment is full of dramatic tension. In the wake of the dangerous and tricky women of Odysseus's journey, of Agamemnon's warnings about faithless wives, of the song of Aphrodite's adultery with Ares, and of Penelope's own possibly ambiguous act in soliciting bridal gifts (book 18) before she knows of Odysseus's return, the simile poses a question to Penelope. Her reply shows a clear perception of and assent to the model of kingship suggested by Odysseus, if she does not yet recognize her husband. We have seen the Suitors awed by her beauty, and heard them paying tribute to her

remarkable skill and cleverness. Yet Penelope now repeats her disclaimer
that her fame, beauty, and excellence have been lost in the absence of
Odysseus and goes on later in their conversation to describe how through
chastity and care for Odysseus's goods and family she has circumspectly
attempted to preserve his place (19.124–27 and 524–29):

> Stranger, all of my excellence, my beauty and my figure,
> were ruined by the immortals at that time when the Argives
>   took ship
> for Ilion, and with them went my husband, Odysseus.
> If he were to come back and take care of my life, then
> my reputation would be more great and splendid.
> . . . .
> so my mind is divided and starts one way, then another.
> Shall I stay here by my son and keep all in order,
> my property, my serving maids, and my high-roofed house,
> keep faith with my husband's bed and regard the voice of
>   the people,
> or go away at last with the best of all those Achaians
> who court me here in the palace, with endless gifts to woo
>   me?
>
> (Translated by Richmond Lattimore)

She accepts Odysseus's compliment to her abilities by taking pride in her
own exemplary—almost, she suggests in her elaboration on her theme,
masculine—treatment of strangers; yet in the same speech she denies that
she is capable of offering full hospitality—gifts, transportation to another
place—without Odysseus (19.309–16, 325–34):

> If only this word, stranger and guest, were brought to
>   fulfillment,
> soon you would be aware of my love and many gifts given
> by me so that any man who met you would call you
>   blessed.
> But here is the way I think in my mind, and the way it will
>   happen.
> Odysseus will never come home again, nor will you be
>   given
> conveyance, for there are none to give orders left in the
>   household
> such as Odysseus was among men—if he ever existed—

for receiving strangers and sending them off on their
    journeys.
. . . .
. . . for how, my friend, will you learn if I in any way
surpass the rest of women, in mind and good sense,
if you must attend, badly dressed and unwashed, the
    feasting
in the palace? Human beings live only for a short time,
and when a man is harsh himself, and his mind knows
    harsh thoughts,
all man pray that sufferings will befall him hereafter
while he lives; and when he is dead all men make fun of
    him.
But when a man is blameless himself, and his thoughts are
    blameless,
the friends he has entertained carry his fame widely
to all mankind, and many are they who call him excellent.
                    (Translated by Richmond Lattimore)

Her response to the stranger tacitly reaffirms the traditional relation of subordination between husband and wife, reaffirms the limits of her own power and the particular forms necessary for social reproduction on Ithaca.

The vision of kingship in the simile implies a complex symbolic connection between government, agriculture, the worship of the gods and human fertility, as well as a special relation of mutual consent between the sexes. Social reproduction in Ithaca involves dealing creatively with change, exchange and conflict. War, the advent of strangers, the quarrels between families, the need for cooperative organization of agriculture to produce food, the succession of father by son in a kingship all demand a particular control over nature and time. Thus the long process of restoration for Odysseus is appropriate to the challenge of reproducing a continuous culture on Ithaca, not a function of Homer's desire to create suspense. Society in Ithaca is more complex than others we encounter in the poem and its restoration must be correspondingly delicate and complex. As P. Vidal-Naquet has pointed out, the world of the travels is radically simplified in the areas most significant to Ithacan culture: agriculture, marriage and social relationships within the family. There is a correspondingly diminished need for kingship, marriage and social hierarchy. Without war or the necessity to organize labor to reproduce agriculture, the attenuated social structures that we find on some of the islands without hierarchy and with a female on top appear perfectly viable. Life in Ithaca is uniquely characterized by a range of mediating structures organized and unified by a male leader. Through Odysseus's travels we recomprehend the complexity of Ithacan culture and the particular form of male-female relations within it.

On Circe's island or Calypso's, for example, economic production in the household alone is sufficient to sustain her limited social world. It is of parenthetical interest to an evaluation of women's role in Greek literature that their work—weaving, cooking and the guardianship of the household—is present even on Olympus and in utopia. Household economics does not require men or the establishment of a sexual hierarchy and women's control over this sphere is seen as natural, unproblematic. The absence of male agricultural work defines the golden age, just as its presence defines the break into culture, into a world ruled by men. Cooking and weaving on Ithaca are activities dependent on prior agricultural production. The household, as in the analysis in Xenophon's *Oeconomicus*, processes and makes useful and permanent goods produced by men through agriculture and herding. Because both cooking and weaving retard or conquer change they logically have a more primary association with the divine and eternal than male-controlled agriculture. Thus the products of weaving are in Homer sometimes forms of art comparable to poems.

As an example, we may contrast the Homeric *oikos* with the cave of the nymphs (13.102ff. and 345ff.) where Odysseus stores his treasures on Ithaca. In this cave the nymphs perform in perpetuity the female functions of an Homeric household. The cave is filled with stone looms, bowls and jars; it protects Odysseus's goods. Here the divine and human intersect; gods and men through separate entrances communicate indirectly through sacrifice. But this cave world of Circe, Calypso and the nymphs with its endless weaving and banqueting admits neither social change or exchange. This is both its value and its limitation. The female protects what is permanent and unchanging in the Homeric oikos, the male its changing place in historical time. Penelope uses powers natural to her sphere when she temporarily transforms Ithaca to a domestic island in which the minimum of change and exchange takes place.

In a similar vein the islands, with the exception of Phaeacia, are too remote to need a foreign policy, to conduct war or to maintain the complex exchanges of favor between host and guest. Yet it is significant that the arrival of the stranger Odysseus, and the experience of the Trojan war he brings with him, radically disrupt the cultural balance of every world which does not reject him with instant hostility. In Ithaca, by contrast, the continual necessity to recognize boundaries, make economic exchange and declare new areas of influence demands the presence of an authoritative male.

Last and most important for our purposes, the islands of Odysseus's travels organize sexual reproduction on a different basis. If Odysseus had accepted Calypso's belated offer of immortality, he would have avoided the necessity of sexual reproduction altogether. Hesiod's Odysseus has offspring by Circe and Calypso. Homer's has none. The gods of the *Odyssey* disapprove of goddesses mating with mortals (5.118ff.). In a similar vein Hesiod's goddesses mate rarely with men. Their offspring are obscure or short-lived. Yet Zeus and the other male gods sire innumerable culture heroes on mortal women. Where culture, as in Ithaca, cannot be reproduced without the male, there is a corresponding emphasis on sexual reproduction through the male. In Hesiod's *Works and Days* agriculture and mortality come to men simultaneously. In a fallen world men reproduce property (through agriculture) and sons to inherit their property. Similarly, Zeus's achievements are more social than biological, although without females he cannot give birth to Athena, or father other children whose names indicate the development of sophisticated social structures (such as *Dike*). In the island worlds of Circe or Calypso, Homer appears to abstract an incomplete "domestic" world from a larger social reality. Insofar as we accept that these worlds fully represent the domestic sphere, the absence of sexual reproduction suggests that in the larger reality women do not culturally reproduce children. Telemachus cannot attain maturity without the support of other men, nor his full inheritance without Odysseus. Apollo in Aeschylus's *Eumenides* makes a similar point when he argues that the father is the only real parent.

Alternatively, in the stable societies of Aeolus and Phaeacia marriages are between familiars (incestuous or endogamous), not between strangers (exogamous). Without war they need not create a complex network of external alliances to protect and reproduce the social order. In Ithaca relations between strangers are of primary importance; marriages are on the same pattern, between strangers. The success of the marriage depends on the consent of the wife to count her husband's interests as her own, and Penelope's creative fidelity is viewed as remarkable. Thus Homer's selection of the contrasting marriage pattern, marriage between familiars, for his utopian society seems appropriate to its isolation from the external world. Similarly, Odysseus's recovery of his natural relations with Telemachus and even with Laertes are relatively brief, while the redevelopment of his relationship with Eumaeus, and more particularly with Penelope, are long delayed and elaborate. Through Eumaeus, Odysseus symbolically recovers an understanding with those men, often originally strangers, who maintain the external economics of his household. In Ithaca kings play an active role in agriculture. In contrast the other Homeric warriors live off the economic surplus of their society in exchange for offering protection; outside Ithaca we thus find little mention of the peasant classes in Homeric society. In sum, by presenting in isolation these aspects of the more complex Ithacan culture, the islands of the travels clarify the nature and range of female power over the inner sphere of household production, and of the male power over the external world of agriculture, diplomacy and exchange.

The two tokens by which Odysseus is united with wife and father demonstrate clearly the special quality of social relationships on Ithaca. Odysseus identifies himself to Laertes by means of an orchard. There he finds unchanged the trees his father planted for him in youth. Odysseus depends on others to accomplish the laborious and deliberate ordering of nature over time necessary to economic reproduction on Ithaca. Yet only Odysseus can assure economic reproduction; without him the products of agriculture and herding are dissipated, not accumulated as wealth. Laertes lives in poverty and isolation; Eumaeus cannot marry; Penelope cannot give gifts.

The secret of Penelope's life with Odysseus is symbolized in their bed. Odysseus built the bed around a living tree trunk. One post is immovable, rooted in nature. Yet the resulting creation is more lasting than nature. Odysseus depends on Penelope to protect this symbol of the internal continuity of the family. Through this power over their bed we see her outmaneuver the ever-crafty Odysseus. While she accepts her renewed sexual subordination to Odysseus, she is not forced to capitulate to him on his own terms. In contrast, Circe fails to trick Odysseus when she uses her power over bed (10.333–35) and food for treacherous purposes.

The long recourting of Penelope by Odysseus, beginning with the simile of the just king and ending with the simile of the sailor, arises in part, as A. Amory has sensitively suggested, from Penelope's psychological reluctance to recognize Odysseus—a reluctance born of her twenty-year vigilance against deception and the protective freezing of her own sexuality. Yet the recourting is primarily a mature renegotiation between two potential strangers, two established powers, which ends in a recreation of trust and a mutual establishment of the limits within which their future relationship will take place. The process begins with Odysseus's tacit recognition of Penelope's role in preserving his kingship, and his testing of her apparent unwillingness—unlike Clytemnestra—to misuse her power. This hint of dangerous potential sexual inversion shapes our reading of the rewooing of Penelope by Odysseus. Shakespeare's Rosalind also ends by consenting to her marital subordination to Orlando at the close of *As You Like It*. Yet what has passed between them in the period of disguise is surely not irrelevant to our sense of the outcome. Rosalind has won for herself no ordinary wifehood, however it may appear, as the couple joins a throng of other newlyweds at the end of the play. Similarly, by the time Penelope recognizes Odysseus they have, even if subconsciously, recreated the ideal marriage which Odysseus describes to Nausicaa in book 6, lines 180–85:

> and then may the gods give you every thing that your heart
>   longs for;
> may they grant you a husband and a house and sweet
>   agreement
> in all things, for nothing is better than this, more steadfast
> than when two people, a man and his wife, keep a
>   harmonious
> household; a thing that brings much distress to the people
>   who hate them
> and pleasure to their well-wishers, and for them the best
>   reputation.
>   (Translated by Richmond Lattimore)

Despite his initial caution Odysseus comes to rely completely on Penelope's stratagems to set the stage for his revenge. Their final reunion takes place not on his terms but hers: she accepts not the bloody man of force but the verbal and orderly man of peace; she controls the token of the bed. Her feelings about her dream in which the eagle destroys her pet geese (19.536–50), her winning of gifts from the Suitors, and her establishment of the contest with the bow before she knows of Odysseus's return are not consciously intended as hostile to her husband. Yet she weeps at the slaughter of the geese and feels frightened and angry at the eagle. Again, while Odysseus dreams of a mature Penelope supporting him with full recognition of his identity, Penelope dreams of the young Odysseus before he went to Troy. They dream together; yet the two images still separate man and wife. The images converge only in their final reunion. In the simile of the shipwrecked sailor Penelope takes on the mature Odysseus's experiences as her own. They meet again in a new present as she finally breaks her almost enchanted attachment to the past, to the stopping of change which was her central weapon. Penelope's dreams and dreamlike decisions reflect simultaneously her emerging acceptance of Odysseus's return and her instinctive reluctance to relinquish full control over the household. By eschewing her opportunity for usurping or misusing power Penelope secures from her husband a different kind of power and a marriage clarified by their mutual recognition of like-mindedness.

Odysseus's experiences with Nausicaa and Arete on Phaeacia prepare us to understand the importance of the form of negotiation between husband and wife and the nature of the outcome. In Phaeacia the figure of Arete is mysteriously central. Alcinous holds the power (*kratos*). Arete, relying on her husband's reverence for her, and accepting her subordination to him, is allowed the limited public role of resolving disputes between the husbands of wives who are in her favor (7.73–74). Yet Odysseus is twice advised to make his pleas to her alone. Bernard Fenik has gone far in exploring this question. He suggests that Arete's importance emerges in one particular scene, the scene where she tests Odysseus with questions about his clothing. Phaeacians are reportedly suspicious of strangers. We are thus prepared dramatically for Odysseus's fate to depend on his answer to this awkward question. Odysseus shows himself, as he did earlier with Nausicaa, to be the ideally tactful man, and Arete is presumably satisfied. Yet Odysseus woos her again in his tale of the underworld by featuring his reunion with his mother and the stories of famous wives. Silence follows the ensuing pause in his story. Then Arete proposes that more gifts be given to Odysseus. The disguised Odysseus makes a comparable indirect compliment to Penelope when he describes the cloak worn by Odysseus in a fictional encounter on Crete. There he emphasizes how impressed the other women were at the workmanship of the cloak (19.234–35).

Alcinous—like Menelaus at Sparta—is more satisfied by appearances than his wife. But even in the most civilized contexts the basis for agreement and understanding between men and women remains problematic. The complexity of these negotiations of the inner domestic world—later perfected in the novel—seem to strain Homer's stylistic repertoire. Interpreters of the scenes between Odysseus and Arete, Odysseus and Penelope, or Helen and Menelaus have turned to an analysis of a variety of stylistic devices such as type-scenes or patterns of repetition for clarification of their unspoken logic. Homer uses and may even have further developed the reverse simile and the dream to express more precisely the ambiguity of Penelope's position and her inner life. Similarly, the obliquely uncomplimentary tales of Helen and Menelaus, and the presence of drugs at their court subtly express uneasy relations in the domestic realm at Sparta. In contrast Odysseus's tact and skill with words neutralizes the potential uneasiness of his relation with Arete and her daughter.

At Ithaca the like-mindedness of Odysseus and Penelope is continually recreated through the long recognition process. Through this like-mindedness women like Arete and Penelope win from their husbands influence even in the external world of their society. The woman's consent is in both cases shown to be essential to the male's success in ruling, and it must be won with a special form of gentle, uncoercive negotiation. Odysseus, contrary to Agamemnon's advice in the underworld or Telemachus's rough manners with his mother, is consistently kind (*ēpios*), not forceful to Penelope. In both Phaeacia and Ithaca Homer gives the central place to Odysseus's ability to be indirect and graceful in his dealings with women. If this is not fully borne out in the case of Arete, it is with Penelope. Arete's role probably also prefigures Penelope's in a restored Ithaca. I see no reason to assume, from Telemachus's adolescent attempts to break out from his mother's influence, that Penelope is to live the rest of her life isolated in the women's quarters. Rather she will take her turn at giving gifts (see 19.309–11) and receiving visitors publicly at Odysseus's side. Like Arete she has won her husband's trust and shown her ability to settle disputes even among men.

This mode of complex and indirect negotiation for male-female relations in the poem becomes in Ithaca symbolic of an important dimension of Odysseus's kingship. Ithacan culture requires a comparable subtly established like-mindedness between the king and his domestic and agricultural subordinates like Eumaeus, Eurycleia, the bard and the herald. The apparent lack of contradiction in the poem between recovering oikos and state (the second mysteriously and abruptly accomplished by Athena-ex-machina) suggests that we can interpret Odysseus's elaborate recovery of his marriage and family as symbolic of a wider restoration of his kingdom on the same pattern. Because the marriage is, as here, apparently used to express a larger range of hierarchical relations between

"strangers" in the society, women have, not surprisingly, a correspondingly powerful and highly valued social and ideological position in the
poem.

In order to evaluate fully the reverse-sex similes we must briefly
return to an examination of the role of inversion in the structure of
Odysseus's journey as a whole. Odysseus gains understanding of Ithaca,
an ever-increasing desire for home and Penelope, and a renewed social
flexibility through his experience of the incompletely human. Odysseus
tests all the limits of his culture. He rejects the choice of becoming a
god. He enters and returns from the world of the dead. At one moment
he is nameless, without identity; at another he is already the hero of
undying fame (Phaeacia). With Nausicaa he has the opportunity to relive
a youthful marriage. On Ithaca he experiences before his time the in-
dignity of poverty and old age. He explores the full range of nuances in
the host-guest relationship. He visits cultures which, because of their
isolation from war or their lack of need for agricultural or sexual reproduction offer him no social function he can recognize and accept. Odysseus never experiences the ultimate reversal from male to female. Yet
numerous critics have commented on Odysseus's special ability to comprehend and respond to the female consciousness, on his "non-mascu-
line" heroism and on his and Penelope's special affinity with the
androgenous Athena. The simile comparing Odysseus to a woman weeping over her dead husband in war (8.523–31) perhaps suggests how close
Odysseus has come in the course of his travels, and in particular on
Calypso's island, to the complete loss of normal social and emotional
function which is the due of women enslaved in war. The earlier comparison of Penelope to an entrapped lion suggests her beleagured position
in Ithaca, and thus resonates with this simile as well. Once conqueror of
Troy, Odysseus now understands the position of its victims; and it is as
such a victim, aged, a beggar, and no longer a leader of men, that he
reenters Ithaca.

On Circe's island his men flock around Odysseus like calves about
their mother (10.410–15), and in recovering Odysseus they feel they have
symbolically recovered Ithaca (10.416–17). Yet Odysseus is not Ithaca;
and in his journey to the underworld he rediscovers how much of his
identity depends not only on his own heroic and warlike powers but on
mothers, fathers, sons, and wives. Ithaca, too, cannot fully reproduce
itself without Odysseus. The cluster of reverse similes surrounding the
return of Odysseus reinforce and clarify the nature of this interdependence of identity in his own culture. Odysseus regains his son and father

by sharing action and work. Yet the key to his return is and has been Penelope. With Penelope he recreates mutual trust both verbally and through a gradual and delicate reawakening of sexual feeling. The characteristics associated with both the male sphere—with its special relation to war as well as agriculture—and with the female sphere—weaving and maintaining the domestic environment—are each shown to be potentially unstable in one dimension. Odysseus's warlike virtues did not provide a safe return for his men, and sometimes, as with the Cyclops, they are directly responsible for their deaths; his armed presence violates the cultural balance of many peaceful islands on his journey. In contrast, he recovers Ithaca not merely through carefully meditated violence, but also through indirection and gentle persuasion. Conversely, uncontrolled female sexuality or irresponsible guardianship of the domestic environment are directly destructive to the cultural order of Ithaca. Yet I would emphasize here that Homer is not criticizing these "male" or "female" powers per se. Purely warlike qualities are appropriate at Troy. Circe's behavior is not inappropriate to a world where agriculture is automatic and foreign policy can be conducted by magic. After all, without the weapon of her sexuality Penelope could not have preserved Ithaca for Odysseus. Instead the poem argues the necessary limitation of each for a stable Ithacan culture.

Thus the *Odyssey* argues for a particular pattern of male-female relations within Ithaca. The reverse similes which frame the return of Odysseus reinforce and explore these interdependent relationships. The two famous similes comparing Penelope to an Odysseus-figure accomplish this purpose with particular subtlety. In contrast to the *Iliad,* where such reverse-sex similes cluster randomly around the relation of Patroclus and Achilles, the Odyssean similes are integral to the structural development of the poem. Penelope's restraint in preserving Odysseus's kingship without usurping his power reveals the nature of her own important guardianship of the domestic sphere. During the period of tacit negotiation which takes place before their final recognition, Odysseus and Penelope recreate a mature marriage with well-defined spheres of power and a dynamic tension between two like-minded members of their sex.

Odysseus: Name and Helmet

Jenny Strauss Clay

κερδαλέος κ' εἴη καὶ ἐπίκλοπος ὅς σε παρέλθοι
ἐν πάντεσσι δόλοισι.

He would have to be a sly one and a thievish rogue, who could surpass you in all your wiles.

(13.291–92)

Our preliminary study of the proem has raised more questions than it has answered. The poet's awareness of his privileged position as mediator between gods and men, the purposeful structuring of his narrative, and the portrayal of his enigmatic hero—these are some of the strands that emanate from the proem, and these are the red threads we must follow through the labyrinth of the poem. At its center is Odysseus, the man of many wiles, whose most characteristic trait is "the fundamental ambiguity of his essential qualities." We must exercise patience and dexterity to track and perhaps to capture this elusive figure. For *metis* does not yield to frontal assault but escapes from our grasp like the ghosts of Hades or the varied shapes of Proteus. Comprehension of the multiplicity of Odysseus demands a multiple and sometimes indirect approach. His name and origins, certain objects with which he is closely associated, and his relation to other heroes provide varied perspectives on this most complex and intriguing figure of Greek literature.

THE NAME OF ODYSSEUS

Language, modern linguists assure us, is an arbitrary system of signs. The Greeks were not so sure. The debate between those who

---

From *The Wrath of Athena*. © 1983 by Princeton University Press. The notes have been omitted.

maintain that language is purely conventional and their opponents who believe that language is "by nature" has a long history which cannot be traced here. But most early etymological speculation presupposes that a name and the thing denominated are closely related, i.e., that a name, correctly understood, indicates the nature of the thing named. The fact that many Greek proper names have transparent meanings (e.g., Aristodemus "Best-of-the-people," Telemachus "Far-fighter," and Patroclus "Glory-of-the-father") lends powerful support to such a view. The more opaque names and epithets of the most mysterious of beings, the gods, and the famous heroes of the past tease the ingenuity of the Greeks from the earliest times. When Sappho ponders the meaning of Hesperus, the evening star, or when Aeschylus has the Chorus of the *Agamemnon* pause to reflect on the name of Helen (ll. 689–90), or when, in the same play, Cassandra recognizes the source of her destruction in the name of Apollo (ll. 1080ff.), they are not indulging in mere punning or wordplay. Rather, they manifest a time-honored conviction that a proper understanding of a name will reveal the hidden nature of what the name designates. Such a name is called an *onoma eponumon,* a name that corresponds appropriately to the person or object designated. Homer and Hesiod offer numerous examples of this kind of etymological thinking, and it is not surprising that Homer should allow himself to speculate about the meaning of the name of Odysseus.

Our attention has already been drawn to that name indirectly through its omission in the proem, which introduced an anonymous hero whose polytropic character is revealed in his passive ability to endure great suffering and in his active role as the man of metis. The same double perspective is retained at the end of the poem. After Odysseus and Penelope are finally reunited and have taken their pleasure in lovemaking, they each tell their stories. Odysseus's summary of his long travels and adventures—of his Odyssey—is introduced as follows:

> αὐτὰρ ὁ διογενὴς Ὀδυσεὺς ὅσα κήδε᾽ ἔθηκεν
> ἀνθρώποις ὅσα τ᾽ αὐτὸς ὀϊζύσας ἐμόγησε,
> πάντ᾽ ἔλεγ᾽.

> But Zeus-born Odysseus told her all—all the troubles he set upon men, and all that he himself had suffered in misery.
> (23.306–8)

Troubles inflicted and troubles endured—these are the twofold aspects of the hero. The name itself, Odysseus, embraces both and is profoundly ambiguous in its significance.

Odysseus's naming is recounted within the framework of the famous recognition scene. The old nurse Eurycleia washes the feet of her master, who is still disguised as a beggar (19.361ff.). As she touches the old scar which identifies the stranger as Odysseus, its history is told in a leisurely fashion—how, as a youth, Odysseus visited his maternal grandfather Autolycus and took part in a hunt for a boar on the slopes of Parnassus. The boar attacked and wounded Odysseus who then succeeded in killing the beast. The sons of Autolycus healed the wound, which left the identifying scar, and then sent the young hero home with splendid gifts. The parents rejoiced at the safe and triumphant return of their son, who recounted his adventures with the boar. At this point, the narrative returns to the main story: Eurycleia touches the old scar, recognizes it, and drops the foot of Odysseus into the washbasin with a great splash. Eurycleia's joy at the return of her absent master differs from the parents' simple joy of long ago which accompanied the return of their young son (χαῖρον νοστήσαντι, 19.463); hers is mixed with pain (χάρμα καὶ ἄλγος, 19.471). The old woman's eyes fill with tears and she gasps, "Indeed, you are Odysseus, dear child" (19.474).

Framed within the tale of the boar's hunt and Odysseus's scar—in the manner of Chinese boxes—is the story of Odysseus's naming by his grandfather Autolycus. At first, its connection to the narrative of the scar seems tangential, if not gratuitous. The only apparent link is that the hunt was undertaken in the company of Autolycus and his sons. At any rate, we get a brief description of Autolycus and an account of his earlier visit on the occasion of Odysseus's birth. At that time, Autolycus invited his grandson to visit him when he had grown up, promising to give him many gifts. And so, years later, Odysseus came to Parnassus and earned his scar. What first appear to be purely associative and somewhat rambling digressions turn out to be an exemplary model of the characteristic Homeric technique of ring-composition, in which narrative material is arranged in the general form A B C B A. If ring-composition accounts for the formal structure of this digression, it does not in itself throw light on the organic interconnections of the passage on the level of content. To be sure, the story of how Odysseus acquired his scar follows quite reasonably upon Eurycleia's recognition of the scar, but Odysseus's acquisition of his name appears at first to be unrelated to the overall narrative frame.

In a well-known essay, Erich Auerbach begins his study of the Western tradition of the literary representation of reality by comparing the Homeric epic with biblical narrative. With admirable sensitivity, he contrasts the clarity, fullness, and plasticity of the epic with the inward and elliptical style of biblical storytelling. For all his merits, Auerbach is rather unfortunate in choosing the passage involving Odysseus's scar to exemplify the epic style as "externalized, uniformly illuminated phenomena . . . in a perpetual foreground." He claims that "When the young Euryclea (ll. 401ff.) sets the infant Odysseus on his grandfather Autolycus's lap after the banquet, the aged Euryclea . . . has entirely vanished from the stage and from the reader's mind." Auerbach seems to forget that only Eurycleia, who was Odysseus's nurse and present at his naming, could pronounce the words

$$\text{ἦ μάλ' Ὀδυσσεύς ἐσσι, φίλον τέκος.}$$

You indeed are Odysseus, dear child.
(19.474)

The formula in this line has occurred only twice before in the *Odyssey*. At the moment Circe recognizes Odysseus as *polytropos,* she exclaims:

$$\text{ἦ σύ γ' Ὀδυσσεύς ἐσσι πολύτροπος.}$$

You indeed are *polytropos* Odysseus.
(10.330)

The formula is to be found once more, when Telemachus *denies* that the strange beggar suddenly beautified by Athena can be his father:

$$\text{οὐ σύ γ' Ὀδυσσεύς ἐσσι πατὴρ ἐμός.}$$

You indeed cannot be Odysseus, my father.
(16.194)

Yet Odysseus is indeed Telemachus's father, despite such denials; to Circe, he is the man of many turnings; but only for Eurycleia, present at his birth and childhood adventures, does he remain "dear child." Background illuminates foreground. The naming scene belongs within the context of the description of the scar. The name—and the story behind it—identifies Odysseus fully as much as his scar.

Odysseus's maternal grandfather, Autolycus, whose name suggests something like Lone Wolf, comes to Ithaca to name the infant. Eurycleia places the child on Autolycus's lap and urges him to choose a name for his grandson. Tactfully, she suggests "Polyaretus" or "Much-Prayed-for." But Autolycus has other ideas:

γαμβρὸς ἐμὸς θυγάτηρ τε, τίθεσθ᾽ ὄνομ᾽ ὅττι κεν εἴπω·
πολλοῖσιν γὰρ ἐγώ γε ὀδυσσάμενος τόδ᾽ ἱκάνω,
ἀνδράσιν ἠδὲ γυναιξὶν ἀνὰ χθόνα πουλυβότειραν·
τῷ δ᾽ Ὀδυσεὺς ὄνομ᾽ ἔστω ἐπώνυμον.

My son-in-law and daughter, give the name I say:
for I come here a curse (*odyssamenos*) to many
men and women all over the much-nurturing earth;
therefore let his name appropriately be Odysseus.

(19.406–9)

Autolycus derives the name Odysseus from the verb *odysasthai*, which means "to have hostile feelings or enmity toward someone." The word embraces a range of meanings, including "to be angry," "to hate someone," "to vex," "to trouble," "to offend." A few translators have attempted to bring the play on words over into English. Fitzgerald translates: "odium and distrust I've won. Odysseus / should be his given name;" Lattimore renders it as follows: "since I have come to this place distasteful to many . . . so let him be given / the name Odysseus, that is distasteful." Giving up on the pun, I have translated *odyssamenos* as "a curse" to bring out the fact that the name Autolycus chooses is the very opposite of the one the nurse proposes. Eumaeus, the faithful swineherd, seems to allude to the ill-omened character of his absent master's name when he speaks of him to the disguised beggar:

τὸν μὲν ἐγών, ὦ ξεῖνε, καὶ οὐ παρεόντ᾽ ὀνομάζειν
αἰδέομαι· πέρι γάρ μ᾽ ἐφίλει καὶ κήδετο θυμῷ·
ἀλλά μιν ἠθεῖον καλέω καὶ νόσφιν ἐόντα.

Stranger, I am ashamed to name him in his absence.
For he loved me greatly and cared for me in his heart;
instead, I shall call him "dear friend" even if he is far away.

(14.145–47)

This interpretation of Odysseus's name is borne out indirectly by the fictitious name and lineage Odysseus concocts when he introduces himself to his aged father in the last book of the *Odyssey*. There, he calls himself Eperitus, son of Apheidon, grandson of Polypemon (24.305–6). As we might expect, all these names are significant and reveal something about Odysseus's character. Pape-Benseler gives "Strife" as the meaning of Eperitus, but offers no explanation. It seems to derive from ἐπήρεια, "insulting treatment," "abuse," and is possibly related to ἀρειή, "men-

ace," "threat," and Sanskrit *irasya,* "hostility," cf. Latin *ira,* "anger."
Homer may also have incorrectly connected it with ἐπαράομαι, "to
curse." In any case, the name Odysseus manufactures for himself corresponds closely to the meaning of his true name. Apheidon clearly means
"Unsparing" and should, I suggest, not be connected with thrift but
with ruthlessness, a quality not altogether foreign to Odysseus's character. We may remember Eurymachus's plea at the beginning of the
slaughter of the Suitors: "Spare your people" (σὺ δὲ φείδεο λαῶν,
22.54). Mercilessly, Odysseus rejects his entreaty. Finally, Polypemon,
"Much-pain," has the same double sense which conforms to all we have
observed of Odysseus; it can mean both "Suffering-much-pain" and
"Causing-much-pain."

The name of Odysseus is similarly double and my rendering,
"curse," solves the problem of whether Autolycus's odyssamenos should
be taken as active or passive—"angry at many" or "incurring the anger
of many." In Greek, the verb is in the middle voice, that is, something
between active and passive, which, as Benveniste defines it, is "an act in
which the subject is affected by the process and is himself situated within
the process." This double and reciprocal sense of incurring and dealing
out enmity perfectly suits the trickster Autolycus, of whom we have just
learned:

> ὃς ἀνθρώπους ἐκέκαστο
> κλεπτοσύνῃ θ' ὅρκῳ τε. θεὸς δέ οἱ αὐτὸς ἔδωκεν
> Ἑρμείας.

> he surpassed all men
> in thievery and equivocation; and a god gave him this talent,
> Hermes.

> (19.395–97)

"Curse," as I have translated odyssamenos, also has the advantage
of having religious overtones. Such a connotation is singularly fitting,
since elsewhere in Homer odysasthai is used exclusively to designate divine
displeasure or wrath. The verb occurs four times in the *Iliad,* and its
subject is always Zeus or "the gods." The most illuminating passage
involving odysasthai appears in book 6 within the context of the famous
encounter between Diomedes and Glaucus on the battlefield, which ends
with their discovery of ancient ties of hospitality between their families.
The weight of mortality hangs over the meeting. Only a short time before,
Diomedes had wounded both Ares and Aphrodite with Athena's help,

but now he seems unsure whether his new adversary is a god or a mortal. If he should be a god, Diomedes refuses to fight with him. As an example of the dangers consequent to fighting with the gods, Diomedes then recounts the story of Lycourgus who had the temerity to attack Dionysus:

> τῷ μὲν ἔπειτ᾽ ὀδύσαντο θεοὶ ῥεῖα ζώοντες,
> καί μιν τυφλὸν ἔθηκε Κρόνου πάϊς· οὐδ᾽ ἄρ᾽ ἔτι δὴν
> ἦν, ἐπεὶ ἀθανάτοισιν ἀπήχθετο πᾶσι θεοῖσιν.

> Thereafter, the gods who live easy were angered at him,
> and the son of Cronus made him blind, nor did he
> live long, since he was hated by the immortal gods.
> (*Iliad*, 6.138–40)

Therefore, Diomedes concludes, "I would not want to battle with the immortal gods" (*Iliad*, 6.141). The enmity of the gods is aroused by Lycourgus's "contending with the celestial gods" θεοῖσιν ἐπουρανίοισιν ἔριζεν (*Iliad*, 6.131); his punishment is blindness and premature death.

In the *Odyssey* we find—with the sole exception of the Autolycus passage—that odysasthai is consistently limited to the denotation of divine enmity and, more precisely, to the anger of the gods against Odysseus. It occurs in a prominent place of the poem's first scene. Speaking of Odysseus, Athena accuses Zeus: "Why are you so wroth with him?" (τί νύ οἱ τόσον ὠδύσαο, Ζεῦ; 1.62). The goddess employs a form of the same word Autolycus used in naming his grandchild. But here Odysseus is represented, not as one who provokes anger in his fellow men, but as one who undeservedly suffers the wrath of the gods.

Similar plays on Odysseus's name occur three more times in the poem. First, in book 5 the sea nymph Leucothea takes pity on the storm-tossed hero struggling on his raft: "Poor wretch," she says, "why does Poseidon rage (ὠδύσατ᾽) at you so terribly, so that he sows many evils for you?" (5.339–40). Shortly thereafter, when the storm has subsided and land is in sight, Odysseus still fears further mishaps at sea; he says to himself, "I know how much the famous earth-shaker is angered (ὀδώδυσται) at me" (5.423). Finally, in Ithaca, during the first interview between Odysseus and Penelope, the disguised hero announces not only that Odysseus still lives, but also that he is on his way home with many treasures. But, he tells Penelope, the hero's companions have all perished: "for Zeus and Helios were angry (ὀδύσαντο) with him" (19.275–76).

The name of Odysseus, then, reveals itself to have not one but two senses. It refers both to the active Autolycan troublemaker and to the passive victim of divine wrath. As the Man of Wrath, Odysseus both causes trouble and vexation and is much vexed by the hostility of the gods. These two aspects of Odysseus as victim and victimizer coexist side by side and correspond to the same doubleness we have already observed in his identifying epithet, *polytropos*. The doubleness of Odysseus pervades the *Odyssey*.

Yet the *Odyssey* does not exist in a void; it often seems to take its cues from the *Iliad*. It is striking that the twofold meaning of Odysseus's name has a parallel in the name of the hero of the *Iliad*. In a stimulating study of this problem, G. Nagy derives the name of Achilles from ἄχος-λαός, "the man who has grief for and of the people," and shows how the plot of the *Iliad* embodies the meaning of the hero's name. The proem announces the wrath of Achilles which brings "countless woes on the Achaeans," and, in the first book, the Greeks' grief at the plague sent by Apollo leads to Achilles's intervention and the quarrel with Agamemnon. In turn, the *achos,* grief, that the hero suffers on account of his wounded honor brings grief to his people when he withdraws from battle. That grief is momentarily relieved when Achilles sends his friend Patroclus into battle, but the outcome, Patroclus's death, means unceasing grief for Achilles himself. Finally, the lamentation over Patroclus prefigures the grief of the Greeks over Achilles, soon to follow. The plot of the *Iliad* can, then, be meaningfully summarized in that Achilles, the man of sorrow, both suffers grief and inflicts it on his people. According to Nagy's analysis, Achilles's name ends up having a double sense. That name offers a suggestive counterpart to the twofold meaning of the name of Odysseus. It is possible that—like Achilles in his story—the name of Odysseus sums up and defines the plot of his poem. We have already observed that the *Odyssey* begins with the cessation of Athena's wrath. The story of Odysseus, the Man of Wrath, must be understood in terms of his both provoking and incurring wrath.

A further striking and at first puzzling symmetry between the *Iliad* and the *Odyssey* demands attention. With the unique exception of the Autolycus passage, the epic, as we have seen, restricts the subject of the verb odysasthai to the gods. Other words for wrath and anger are shared by both gods and men. The *noun* which corresponds to odysasthai and whose usage in Homer is similarly limited to divine agents is menis. Divine menis is provoked by the breach of certain fundamental rules of human society: there are, for example, sacrifice to the gods (*Iliad*, 5.178, cf. 1.75); hospitality toward strangers and the proper behavior of guests (*Iliad*, 13.624, *Odyssey*, 2.66, 14.283); and due burial of the dead (*Iliad*,

22.358, *Odyssey,* 11.73). In addition, menis is the reaction of the gods to conduct which is superhuman or which tends to erase the distinctions between gods and men. Both Patroclus and Diomedes arouse the menis of Apollo at the moment they are characterized as δαίμονι ἶσος "equal to a *daimon*" (*Iliad,* 16.705, 5.438). In the latter passage Apollo makes explicit the reason for his intervention and warns Diomedes:

φράζεο, Τυδεΐδη, καὶ χάζεο, μηδὲ φεοῖσιν
ἶσ' ἔθελε φρονέειν, ἐπεὶ οὔ ποτε φῦλον ὁμοῖον
ἀθανάτων τε θεῶν χαμαὶ ἐρχομένων τ' ἀνθρώπων.

Take thought, son of Tydeus, and withdraw, nor desire to have
a mind equal to the gods, since never alike is the race
of the immortal gods and of men who walk on the ground.

(*Iliad,* 5.440–42)

In the *Hymn to Aphrodite,* the goddess warns the mortal Anchises to respect the menis of Zeus, who will strike him down with the thunder-bolt if ever Anchises reveals that Aphrodite lay with him and bore his child, Aeneas (ll. 281–90). With the same words (5.146), Hermes warns Calypso to send off Odysseus rather than to keep him as her consort and make him immortal. In every case, menis arises from an attempt to blur or overstep the lines of demarcation separating gods from men.

Elsewhere applied only to the gods, menis is used of only one mortal agent, the wrath of Achilles, the subject of the *Iliad.* Defined in super-human terms, Achilles's wrath makes him more than human. Achilles ascends to an almost divine stature of mimicking and making his own the anger that belongs properly to the gods alone. When the raging Achilles attacks Troy, a simile makes this explicit:

ὡς δ' ὅτε καπνὸς ἰὼν εἰς οὐρανὸν εὐρὺν ἵκηται
ἄστεος αἰθομένοιο, θεῶν δέ ἑ μῆνις ἀνῆκε,
πᾶσι δ' ἔθηκε πόνον, πολλοῖσι δὲ κήδε' ἐφῆκεν,
ὡς Ἀχιλεὺς Τρώεσσι πόνον καὶ κήδε' ἔθηκεν.

As when smoke ascends and comes to wide heaven
of a city in flames, and the wrath of the gods has ignited it,
and it sets toil on all and woe on many;
so did Achilles set toil and woe on the Trojans.

(*Iliad,* 21.522–25)

In the last book of the *Iliad,* the return of Hector's corpse presents Achilles's return to mortality and his acceptance of the rules that govern human society. In his last moments, the dying Hector had begged Achilles to give back his body for burial, and his plea had ended with a threat: "lest I become a cause of divine wrath against you" (*Iliad*, 22.358; cf. the words of Elpenor to Odysseus 11.73). By defiling Hector's corpse and refusing it due burial, Achilles changes from a hero of godlike wrath to a potential object of divine anger (*Iliad*, 24.113–14, 134–35). With the ransoming of Hector and his funeral, the ordered hierarchy between gods and men is restored.

Well and good, but what has all this got to do with the *Odyssey*? The *Odyssey* is obviously a very different kind of poem from the *Iliad*, and Odysseus a very different kind of hero from Achilles. It would be premature at this point to speculate on the nature of those differences. But a preoccupation common to both epics has emerged: in both wrath plays a central role. Watkins has correctly grasped the complex character of menis in the *Iliad*, but his definition is equally valid for the *Odyssey*:

> The association of divine wrath and a mortal by that very fact raises the mortal outside the normal ambiance of the human condition toward the sphere of the divine. . . . We must seek the meaning of μῆνις in the reciprocal relations between gods and men.
>
> ("À propos de menis," *Bull. de la Société de Ling. de Paris* 72, 1977)

Almost by definition, Odysseus is the man who provokes and incurs anger—not only of Poseidon, Helios, and Zeus, but also, as we have seen, of Athena. And of these, only Athena's is called menis (3.135). We will leave for [elsewhere] the question of what constitutes the θεῶν μήνιμα, the cause of divine wrath, against Odysseus. But the menis of Achilles and the name of Odysseus both point to the fact that wrath forms the crucial arena of both poems. Wrath in a sense defines the liminal area between gods and men.

ODYSSEUS AND THE HERITAGE OF AUTOLYCUS

Any discussion of Odysseus's name inevitably leads to a discussion of his relation to Autolycus. Odysseus's genealogical connection with the arch-trickster of the Greek tradition, as well as the many motifs in Odysseus's adventures that offer parallels to widespread folktales, have led scholars to speculate about a pre-Homeric Odysseus who resembles a folklore figure common to almost all peoples. It is the Wily Lad, the folk hero who continually outsmarts and bedevils his opponents with his countless clever tricks and deceptions. Students of the subject maintain that, when this character of popular fantasy was incorporated into the epic tradition, he was purged of some of his more questionable qualities and transformed into a heroic figure. Yet hints and traces of his plebeian origins survive in the *Odyssey*—most clearly in Odysseus's close connection with Autolycus—which do not quite jibe with our expectations of an epic hero, and sometimes even contradict those expectations.

The clearest and most perceptive discussion of this process of the transformation of Odysseus from the hero of folktale to the hero of epic can be found in Maronitis's book. His argument deserves to be taken seriously, if only because it raises some important questions about the interpretation of the Homeric poems. Since his work remains inaccessible even to most classicists because it has not been translated from the Demotic Greek, Maronitis's conclusions are worth summarizing.

Maronitis posits three stages in the evolution of the Odysseus figure: a pre-epic, or what he somewhat unfortunately labels as "novelistic," phase, an epic phase, and finally the Odysseus of the *Odyssey*. In the first, the Odysseus of folklore inherits Autolycus's talents for thievery, especially cattle rustling, and the use of magic spells which allow him to carry out his thefts without being seen or caught. He embodies the gifts of Hermes, the trickster god. During the second stage, Odysseus is incorporated into the epic, particularly into the traditional tales surrounding the Trojan War. Our evidence for the so-called epic cycle is fragmentary and late, but the stories it contained must have preceded the Homeric poems in some form. Odysseus plays an important role in these tales, most spectacularly as the mastermind of the Trojan horse and as the winner in the contest over the arms of Achilles—incidents alluded to in the *Odyssey*. His cleverness and his inherited talent for trickery as well as deceit are, to a certain extent, put to the service of the united Greek cause against the Trojans; but some stories suggest Odysseus's reversion to the old Autolycan freebooter. Finally, in the *Odyssey*, the traditional Odyssean guile is used largely in self-defense and for the preservation of the hero's companions and family. According to Maronitis, the poet of the *Odyssey* has cleansed his hero of the heavy burden of his Autolycan past by suppressing the more unsavory elements of Odysseus's character and reinterpreting negative qualities as positive virtues. The evolution of the figure of Odysseus can be summed up in the change in the meaning of Odysseus's name from the primitive Autolycan sense of the trickster—who causes trouble and vexation for his fellowmen and who provokes the hostility and distaste of decent people everywhere—to the Odyssean Odysseus who is, above all, the long-suffering victim of the undeserved and excessive anger of the gods.

Maronitis's scheme has much to recommend it. No one can doubt that his account of the evolution of the figure of Odysseus goes a long way to explain the development of the most complex and contradictory hero of the Greeks. Fundamental questions, however, remain. For one thing, the Odysseus of the *Iliad* is far "cleaner" than the hero of the *Odyssey*. Stanford notes that while Odysseus retains his reputation for cleverness in the *Iliad,* "his conduct is scrupulously honest and his words are studiously candid. If the *Iliad* were the only early record of Odysseus's career one would find it hard to understand how he had got his notoriety as a man of extreme wiliness. In contrast the *Odyssey* is a compendium of Ulyssean and Autolycan cunning." Perhaps Stanford overstates the case, but if the heroic environment of the *Iliad* has already partially purified Odysseus, then presumably the poet of the *Odyssey* could have continued the process of banishing the skeletons in the closet of Odysseus's past. But he did not, nor did he wish to do so.

The doubleness of Odysseus pervades his poem. It can be found in his name, in his characteristic epithets, but, above all, it informs his words and deeds. It is no accident that, after the prologue, the very first image presented of Odysseus is the most questionable and disturbing one in the entire *Odyssey*. Disguised as Mentes, Athena evokes for Telemachus an earlier meeting with Odysseus:

εἰ γὰρ νῦν ἐλθὼν δόμου ἐν πρώτῃσι θύρῃσι
σταίη, ἔχων πήληκα καὶ ἀσπίδα καὶ δύο δοῦρε,
τοῖος ἐὼν οἷόν μιν ἐγὼ τὰ πρῶτ' ἐνόησα
οἴκῳ ἐν ἡμετέρῳ πίνοντά τε τερπόμενόν τε,
ἐξ Ἐφύρης ἀνιόντα παρ' Ἴλου Μερμερίδαο·
οἴχετο γὰρ καὶ κεῖσε θοῆς ἐπὶ νηὸς Ὀδυσσεὺς
φάρμακον ἀνδροφόνον διζήμενος, ὄφρα οἱ εἴη
ἰοὺς χρίεσθαι χαλκήρεας· ἀλλ' ὁ μὲν οὔ οἱ
δῶκεν, ἐπεί ῥα θεοὺς νεμεσίζετο αἰὲν ἐόντας,
ἀλλὰ πατήρ οἱ δῶκεν ἐμός· φιλέεσκε γὰρ αἰνῶς.

Would that he would come now and stand at the outer gates
    of his house,
with helmet, shield, and two spears,
being the same as when first I knew him
in our house, drinking and enjoying himself

on his return from Ephyra and Ilos, the son of Mermerus;
for Odysseus had gone there on a swift ship,
in search of a man-killing drug, so that he would have it
to smear on his bronze arrows; but Ilos refused
to give it, since he feared the gods who live forever;
but my father gave it to him, for he loved him terribly.

(1.255–64)

This first picture of Odysseus arouses our unease and suspicions, and the context makes clear that decent Homeric society also took offense at the use of poison arrows. To put it mildly, no overrefined sense of fair play encumbers the Odysseus presented here.

The evolutionary explanation of the development of the Odysseus figure is open to a crucial objection. It tends to simplify and hence to flatten the complexities of Odysseus's character as Homer presents them by assigning certain traits to earlier and others to later strata. Such simplification becomes apparent in Maronitis's demonstrations of what he calls the transformations of Odysseus. In one case, Maronitis maintains that the encounter between Odysseus and Ajax (11.543–67) is intended to absolve Odysseus of blame for Ajax's suicide after their contest over the arms of Achilles. According to some traditions, Odysseus won by less than honorable—one might call them Autolycan—means, causing Ajax to go mad and kill himself. The humane and generous words Odysseus addresses to the silent Ajax, with their verbal echoes of the Iliadic quarrel between Achilles and Agamemnon, tend to relieve Odysseus of the burden of guilt and suspicion which characterized other traditions of his victory. There is undoubtedly much truth in Maronitis's interpretation, but he skirts some of the more questionable implications of the meeting of these former antagonists. After all, Ajax remains silent and unforgiving as he goes off among the Dead. Yet Odysseus claims:

ἔνθα χ᾽ ὁμῶς προσέφη κεχολωμένος, ἤ κεν ἐγὼ τόν·
ἀλλά μοι ἤθελε θυμὸς ἐνὶ στήθεσσι φίλοισι
τῶν ἄλλων ψυχὰς ἰδέειν κατατεθνηώτων.

Then, nevertheless, he would have spoken, even though
    angry, or I to him;
but the heart in my own breast desired
to see the souls of others who had died. ⏤

(11.565–67)

Maronitis is obliged to admit that the close of the scene constitutes something of an enigma, but it is more than that. Ajax's unforgiving silence rekindles our suspicions. A number of other things accentuate our malaise: Odysseus's cocky assurance of his eventual success, his rather lame excuse for breaking off the encounter, and the curiosity that triumphs over his desire to make his peace with Ajax. Elsewhere, that curiosity regularly characterizes Odysseus; on occasion, it even endears him to us; here, it strikes one as slightly ignoble. Nor does any suggestion of reconciliation allay our unease. The final impression of this scene and Odysseus's role in it remain ambivalent.

Maronitis's analysis of the Polyphemus episode is open to similar objections. According to him, that episode forms the crowning step in the process of purification of Odysseus from his Autolycan heritage. Here, the Autolycan characteristics—cleverness, trickery, and deception—are transformed from negative to positive qualities. They cease to be purely self-aggrandizing and self-serving; instead, they are put to the service of defensive and communal virtues. Odysseus's *doloi* are employed exclusively to bring about his own and his comrades' escape from the cannibal's cave. This adventure, then, is pivotal, for it results in Odysseus's becoming the object of Poseidon's unjust wrath, odyssamenos. Here, however, Maronitis neglects what cannot be neglected: the beginning of the episode. How did Odysseus get trapped in the monster's cave in the first place? Autolycan curiosity and greed played a critical role in creating Odysseus's predicament. One cannot overlook it with impunity. In sum, the diachronic view of the genesis of Odysseus requires us to ignore some traits at the expense of others and to gloss over inherent contradictions.

The whitewash of Odysseus in the *Odyssey* remains incomplete. The heritage of Autolycus may be played down to a certain extent, but it is by no means completely suppressed. Developmental explanations may help to explain how Odysseus got that way, but they finally interfere with a full understanding of Odysseus as the hero of the *Odyssey*. Once we have separated Odysseus into primitive Autolycan and more progressive "heroic" strata, we can no longer grasp the complex but highly integrated whole whose character is delineated by its very multiplicity.

The Heritage of Autolycus: The Boar's-Tusk Helmet

After having failed to discover a satisfactory account of the Autolycan aspects of Odysseus's character within a developmental framework, we are still faced with the initial question. How should Odysseus's relationship to Autolycus be defined; to what extent is Odysseus true to his name and heir to the Autolycan character of the man who named him? To reject an evolutionary answer to a valid and important question—one that the Homeric text itself raises—is to become responsible for an alternative solution. The only safe and sure approach to such a solution is the venerable principle of "interpreting Homer from Homer." A passage from book 10 of the *Iliad,* the so-called Doloneia, and the only other epic passage that links Autolycus and Odysseus, suggests an answer to our question. To a certain extent, this answer confirms the speculation of scholars concerning the development of the Odysseus figure. However, it does so in Homeric terms which are at once simple and subtle. What is more important, it preserves the integrity of Odysseus's character.

At the beginning of the Doloneia, the most "Odyssean" book of the *Iliad*—and, characteristically, the only one to take place wholly at night—the embassy to persuade Achilles to return to battle has just failed. Agamemnon lies sleepless and anxious, then calls together the Greek chieftains. When an expedition to spy on the Trojan camp is proposed, Diomedes volunteers and chooses Odysseus as his companion. In the meantime, the Trojans too have sent out a spy, Dolon, to discover the intentions of the Greeks. The nocturnal foray itself falls into two parts. It begins with the capture of Dolon; there follows the bloody attack on the sleeping Rhesus and his Thracians, a massacre that leads to the capture of Rhesus's splendid horses. The second incident belongs properly to Diomedes, the first, to Odysseus—as becomes evident from the distribution of the booty after the triumphant return of the heroes. Diomedes gets the Thracian horses (*Iliad,* 10.566–69); Odysseus, the spoils of Dolon (*Iliad,* 10.570–71).

It is ironically appropriate that Odysseus, the man of doloi par excellence, should be pitted against an opponent named Dolon. The Doloneia as a whole is constructed on a pattern of contrast, parallelism, and reversal of expectations, a veritable "game of antitheses." So, the greedy and insane boastfulness of Dolon, who demands the horses of Achilles as his reward for spying on the Greeks, contrasts mightily with the unusual and uncharacteristic modesty of Odysseus, who not only does not set a price on his participation in the venture, but also demurely rejects the praise Diomedes heaps upon him, by saying that "the Greeks already know those things" (*Iliad,* 10.250). The Greeks, moreover, go forth on their mission with no particular goal or ambition, but return with the superb horses of Rhesus, while Dolon not only fails to win his prize, but loses his life as well. In short, the trickster, Dolon, is outtricked.

A similar significance informs the bizarre outfits of the leading actors of the Doloneia. The costumes are appropriate to the character of their wearers. For his spying mission, Dolon dons a wolf skin and a weasel cap, underlining his own disastrous combination of low cunning and insatiable greed. Earlier, Menelaus had put on a leopard skin, while both Agamemnon and Diomedes wear lion pelts. As Reinhardt notes, the relation between Agamemnon and Menelaus, which is touchingly revealed in the king's concern for his beloved but weaker brother (*Iliad,* 10.237–40), finds a subtle expression in their respective outfits. The lion, for the Greeks as for us, embodies heroic majesty, while the leopard, for all his attractiveness, is a creature of a lesser stature. Elsewhere, it is, of course, Paris, Menelaus's rival, who wears the leopard skin (*Iliad,* 3.17). Diomedes, who represents the best qualities of heroic arete in those books in which Achilles is absent, is likewise well suited to the lion skin he wears. Finally, for the raid itself, Odysseus puts on a helmet that introduces yet another animal emblem. For this helmet is made of boar's tusks and described in unusual detail. If the costumes of the other characters in the Doloneia have an emblematic value suitable to their wearers, then Odysseus's helmet must, on the contrary, be understood as a disguise. For the hero of supreme guile encounters his adversary, Dolon, not, as we might expect, in the guise of a fox or a wolf, but as a wild boar, the beast who is known in the similes of the epic as the animal most violent in destructive rage and might. But just as Odysseus plays the fool when addressing the Trojans (*Iliad,* 3.216–24), thus disarming his audience, he can in the Doloneia be said to dissemble his true character in order to trap his adversary. Such, after all, are the ruses of metis.

The full significance of the boar's-tusk helmet has not yet been exhausted, however, for it has an important bearing on the question of Odysseus's Autolycan heritage. Diomedes and Odysseus have come to the nocturnal conference of the Greeks unarmed and are obliged to borrow equipment from the guards for their expedition. It is from one of them, the Cretan Meriones, that Odysseus borrows a bow and spear as well as the helmet, which is described both in terms of its appearance and its history.

To be sure, several important objects in the Homeric poems, especially armor or weapons, are described by means of their history or genealogy. The most elaborate example of such a genealogy is the famous description of Agamemnon's scepter in book 2 of the *Iliad*:

τὸ μὲν Ἥφαιστος κάμε τεύχων.
Ἥφαιστος μὲν δῶκε Διὶ Κρονίωνι ἄνακτι,

αὐτὰρ ἄρα Ζεὺς δῶκε διακτόρῳ ἀργεϊφόντῃ˙
Ἑρμείας δὲ ἄναξ δῶκεν Πέλοπι πληξίππῳ,
αὐτὰρ ὁ αὖτε Πέλοψ δῶκ᾽ Ἀτρέϊ, ποιμένι λαῶν˙
Ἀτρεὺς δὲ θνῄσκων ἔλιπεν πολύαρνι Θυέστῃ,
αὐτὰρ ὁ αὖτε Θυέστ᾽ Ἀγαμέμνονι λεῖπε φορῆναι,
πολλῇσιν νήσοισι καὶ Ἄργεϊ παντὶ ἀνάσσειν.

Hephaestus made it;
and Hephaestus gave it to Zeus, lord son of Cronus,
and then Zeus gave it to the Guide, slayer of Argus;
and the lord Hermes gave it to Pelops, driver of horses;
and Pelops in turn gave it to Atreus, shepherd of the people,
and Atreus, when he died, left it to Thyestes of many sheep;
but Thyestes in turn left it to Agamemnon to carry,
and to rule over many islands and all of Argos.

(*Iliad*, 2.101–8)

The history of the scepter serves to characterize the kingly stature of its present heir, as Lessing demonstrates in his classic interpretation in the *Laocoön*. Similarly, the ash spear, which Achilles inherits from his father Peleus and which is the only original piece of armor he retains for his final confrontation with Hector, should, according to Shannon, be understood as a symbol of Achilles's mortality. The history of an object may, then, offer more than a merely ornamental anecdote; it may serve to characterize its owner in some important way.

Such it will be shown [elsewhere], is the significance of Odysseus's bow. Indeed, it should not surprise us that the weapon that brings the action of the entire *Odyssey* to its climax is dignified with a complex and meaningful account of its origins. It may, however, seem peculiar that Homer lavishes so much attention on borrowed headgear. The lineage of the helmet runs as follows:

τήν ῥά ποτ᾽ ἐξ Ἐλεῶνος Ἀμύντορος Ὀρμενίδαο
ἐξέλετ᾽ Αὐτόλυκος πυκινὸν δόμον ἀντιτορήσας,
ἐκάνδειαν δ᾽ ἄρα δῶκε Κυθηρίῳ Ἀμφιδάμαντι˙
Ἀμφιδάμας δὲ Μόλῳ δῶκε ξεινήϊον εἶναι,
αὐτὰρ ὁ Μηριόνῃ δῶκεν ᾧ παιδὶ φορῆναι˙
δὴ τότ᾽ Ὀδυσσῆος πύκασεν κάρη ἀμφιτεθεῖσα.

Autolycus once took it from Eleon,
breaking into the close-built house of Amyntor, son of
        Ormenus;

> then, in Scandeia he gave it to Amphidamas of Cythera;
> and Amphidamas gave it to Molos as a guest-gift;
> and he, in turn, gave it to his son Meriones to wear;
> and on this occasion it covered the head of Odysseus.
>
> *(Iliad,* 10.266–71)

The verb used three times to describe the *paradosis* of the helmet is *doke,*
"he gave." But in the first instance, the helmet was no gift; Autolycus
stole it. Only here does Autolycus occur in the *Iliad,* and he is not explicitly identified as Odysseus's grandfather. Stanford rejects the notion
that the poet of the Doloneia was unaware of the connection between
Odysseus and Autolycus, even though "Homer gives no hint here of any
relationship."

> But two other explanations are possible. Homer may not have
> troubled to emphasize a universally known fact: if an English
> historian had to record that Henry VIII wore a helmet which
> Henry VII had once confiscated he would not need to remind
> his readers that these two were father and son. Or else a subtler
> reason may have influenced Homer. He may have deliberately
> avoided any reference to Odysseus's ancestry on the female
> side because it would detract from Odysseus' prestige in the
> conventionally heroic atmosphere of the *Iliad.*

Whatever the reasons for Homer's silence, in our passage, the initial theft
of the helmet reveals Autolycus's character to run true to what we have
heard of him in the *Odyssey*; he excelled all men in thievery and equivocal
oath (κλεπτοσύνῃ θ᾽ ὅρκῳ τε, 19.396). His method of operation remains
the same.

The closest parallel to the elaborate history of the helmet is the
transmission of Agamemnon's scepter, but a comparison reveals important differences. First, unlike the scepter, the helmet is not assigned a
divine origin. Then, too, while the scepter is passed lineally from generation to generation, the helmet moves laterally from person to person
with no apparent design. In its wanderings, the helmet proceeds from
Eleon to Cythera, to Crete, and finally, to Troy, whereas the scepter
remains a possession of the royal house and becomes a symbol of the
latter. The scepter, then, symbolizes Agamemnon's kingly inheritance.
The boar's-tusk helmet also describes a legacy but of a rather different
kind: Odysseus's inheritance of those Autolycan characteristics he re-

ceived from his grandfather. With a "natural" transmission along family lines, Odysseus might well have inherited the helmet. In fact, the helmet has had a more complicated and checkered history, but finally it has reached its "natural" heir, Odysseus. A scholiast notes this mysterious coincidence: "It is a pretty reversal that the helmet, having gone through so many hands, again covers the offspring of Autolycus."

It is tempting to speculate on the significance of this bizarre coincidence. An apparently random chain of events turns out to make unexpected sense, one that suggests that there is a kind of order in the world which is hidden but also meaningful. Heraclitus, the most famous ancient proponent of such a hidden ordering of the cosmos, inevitably comes to mind. One of his fragments which "might . . . be taken as a general title for Heraclitus's philosophical thought" fits the present case perfectly: "The invisible harmony is stronger than the visible one" (ἁρμονίη ἀφανὴς φανερῆς κρείττων). However that may be, the curious tale of the helmet suggests that Odysseus's Autolycan heritage is not simple and linear, but complex and indirect. We may conclude that Autolycan qualities are in some sense present in the grandson, but that they are at least partly transmuted.

With the boar's-tusk helmet and its history, the poet gives us a concrete emblem of the relation between Autolycus and Odysseus. Once this overall significance has been grasped, we may try to examine the intervening steps in the helmet's transmission in the hope that they will reveal more about the character of Odysseus's Autolycan heritage. In this respect, however, the internal Homeric evidence is admittedly scant. Amyntor, from whom Autolycus originally stole the helmet, occurs in book 9, lines 448ff. in the *Iliad* as Phoenix's father, who cursed his son for sleeping with his concubine. Then Amyntor set up a guard of his kinsmen to keep Phoenix imprisoned in the house, but on the tenth day Phoenix finally managed to escape. It is intriguing to consider that Phoenix, Amyntor's son, had trouble getting out of the very same house that Autolycus had previously broken into with apparent ease. Homer tells us nothing more about Amphidamas nor about Molos, except that the latter was Meriones's father. There are, however, some later and fragmentary post-Homeric traditions that are suggestive, especially those about Autolycus. But caution and a healthy dose of skepticism must accompany their use, for while it is clear that countless traditional tales stand behind Homer and must have been common knowledge to his audience, any attempt at their recovery opens unto the realm of surmises rather than certainties. With that caveat, I believe it is possible to put together not, indeed, a complete picture, but at least a suggestive outline concerning the origins of the mysterious helmet.

The traditions concerning Autolycus link him closely to Hermes. In the *Odyssey,* as we have seen, Hermes grants Autolycus his thievish talents, but elsewhere the god is not only Autolycus's patron, but also his father. Hermes's name is absent from the helmet passage in the *Iliad,* but his influence can be detected in the rare verb, ἀντιτορέω, to pierce or bore through, which describes Autolycus's break-in to the house of Amyntor. In the *Hymn to Hermes,* the god's characteristic activity is precisely this "boring through." There, Apollo says of Hermes:

πολλάκις ἀντιτοροῦντα δόμους εὖ ναιετάοντας
ἔννυχον οὔ χ' ἕνα μοῦνον ἐπ' οὐδεῖ φῶτα καθίσσαι
σκευάζοντα κατ' οἶκον ἄτερ ψόφου.

Often you have bored through prosperous houses
at night and brought more than one man down,
gathering his goods without a sound.

(ll. 283–85)

Earlier, Hermes himself had threatened to rob the rich shrine of Apollo at Delphi: "I myself will go to pierce through the great house of Pytho" (εἶμι γὰρ εἰς Πυθῶνα μέγαν δόμον ἀντιτορήσων, l. 178). Autolycus's method of breaking and entering is identical to that of Hermes, and like his patron, Autolycus is known as a virtuoso cattle rustler and thief. He is also said to have the power to make himself and other things invisible— a useful talent in his line of work. Now tradition has it that Hermes has a cap of invisibility, which on one occasion at least he lent to Perseus when the latter went off to kill the Gorgon. In the *Iliad* (5.844–45), Athena puts on a similar cap to make herself invisible to Ares. Could the boar's-tusk helmet in our passage in some sense "stand for" the magic cap of invisibility?

An answer to this question requires us to follow the advice of Kuiper: "Whoever wishes to investigate the true nature of this cap made of leather [*Iliad,* 10.261–62] must enter the far reaches of mythology." The dearth of evidence precludes absolute certainty in such an investigation, but what evidence there is does not seem to contradict our conclusion. Two additional points deserve mention. Of Scandeia and Amphidamas, the next link in the transmission of the helmet, nothing more of significance is known. However, an ancient etymology connects Cythera with κευθεῖν, "to hide," so that the name of the island might be interpreted as "hiding place." Furthermore, there is a bizarre notice in Plutarch (*De defectu orac.* 14) referring to a ritual he claims to have witnessed in Crete in which a headless statue, said to be of Molos, was displayed. Headlessness, hiding places, and cap of invisibility—they all add up to an intriguing pattern whose general significance can still be retrieved, even if some of the details remain lost to us. We should remember in this context that Dolon dies by decapitation. It may be considered corroborating evidence, or at least an indication that the present interpretation is on the right track, that Gernet, who approaches the Doloneia from a completely different angle, detects the same nexus of associations in the figure of Dolon: animal disguises, hiding, headlessness, and invisibility.

When we turn to the final link in the chain of transmission, we reach more solid ground. The *Iliad* itself offers ample information concerning Meriones—a Cretan warrior not quite of the first rank—which can be shaped into a plausible portrait. Meriones is first mentioned in the Catalogue of Ships as leader of the Cretans along with Idomeneus (*Iliad,* 2.651). At the mustering of the troops in book 4, Idomeneus marshals the forward ranks, while Meriones takes charge of the rear (*Iliad,* 4.254)—which suggests that Meriones is Idomeneus's junior partner. At times a near equal to the Cretan chieftain, on other occasions Meriones appears to be merely Idomeneus's vassal or underling (ὀπάων, θεράπων). This apparent contradiction, however, does not require theories of multiple authorship or conflicting sources for its resolution, although such stratagems have been tried. Common sense will serve as well, and the inconsistency is most likely due simply to the differences in the two men's ages. After all, when he is not in the company of Idomeneus, Meriones frequently forms part of a group of younger warriors (e.g., *Iliad,* 9.83, 13.93). In book 13, line 249, Idomeneus calls Meriones "dearest of companions" (φίλταθ' ἑταίρων), an expression that reminds us of the relationship between Achilles and Patroclus (cf. *Iliad,* 19.315). But, unlike Patroclus, Meriones has an independent authority as can be seen from the fact that he does not share Idomeneus's tent. On the contrary, it appears that Meriones's tent lies at some distance from the Cretan leader's, perhaps even at the far end of the Cretan forces. For when Meriones meets Idomeneus, who rebukes him for holding back from battle, Meriones explains that he has lost his spear and is now on the way to get another from his camp "which is not nearby" (*Iliad,* 13.268). Moreover, Meriones has moments of independent glory. A conversation with Idomeneus reveals Meriones's special excellence in ambushes (*Iliad,*

13.249ff.). But Meriones's finest hour occurs during the funeral games for Patroclus; in an upset victory—which astonishes the onlookers—he beats Teucer with a masterful feat of bowmanship and wins the prize (*Iliad*, 23.850ff.). Teucer, who shoots first, manages to snap the cord that holds the bird, but Meriones then hits the bird in its free flight.

The *Odyssey* adds nothing to the above portrait of Meriones, although Nestor says that those who accompanied Idomeneus returned home safely (3.191). Diodorus reports that Idomeneus and Meriones were buried together in Cnossus and were there honored with hero cults. The same author also tells of Meriones's travels to Sicily after the fall of Troy and the foundation there of a rich temple devoted to the Cretan cult of the Mothers. Later tradition offers various accounts of Meriones's genealogy. According to Apollodorus, Meriones's father was a bastard son of Deucalion, Idomeneus's father; that would make Meriones Idomeneus's illegitimate nephew. Diodorus, on the other hand, makes Meriones Idomeneus's cousin by calling both Molos and Deucalion sons of Minos. An odd passage in Alcidamas, *Ulysses* 4, describes the sons of Molos who go to Menelaus for the arbitration of a quarrel concerning their father's inheritance. That tradition presumably considers Meriones and Idomeneus as brothers. All of these accounts of Meriones's background and birth tend to explain the somewhat unusual character of the relationship between Meriones and Idomeneus that emerges from the *Iliad*.

Readers of the *Odyssey* will find this composite picture of Meriones strangely familiar. In fact, it offers striking parallels to certain elements of the Cretan tales told by the disguised Odysseus on his return to Ithaca, especially in his various false accounts of his origins. A brief review of those tales will help to make this clear.

Odysseus gives the following story to Athena in book 13: he had fled from Crete after murdering Orsilochus, the son of Idomeneus, in a night ambush. That was because Orsilochus had tried to deprive him of his due share of the booty from Troy on the grounds that he had not served Idomeneus faithfully; instead, he had led his own contingent (13.257ff.). Later, in book 14, Odysseus introduces himself to Eumaeus as Kastor, illegitimate son of the rich Cretan Hylax. Cut off from his patrimony by the legitimate heirs, Kastor restores his fortunes by way of an advantageous marriage. The gods grant him the courage and daring which proves itself most spectacularly in ambushes. Then war and piracy increased his wealth, until he became a man to be reckoned with among the Cretans. At that point, however, Idomeneus forced him to take an unwilling part in the Trojan expedition (14.192–242). Finally, in his first interview with Penelope in book 19, Odysseus gives yet another account of his origins, presenting himself this time as Aithon, younger brother of Idomeneus, who played host to Odysseus on his way to Troy (19.172–98).

In all these lying tales, the stranger's purported Cretan origins, close relationship, and near equality with Idomeneus all remind us of Meriones. But while Meriones's loyalty to Idomeneus in the *Iliad* is never thrown into question, Odysseus's account to Athena is redolent of insubordination and even criminal treachery toward the Cretan chief. As Kastor, Odysseus again presents himself as an unwilling participant in the Trojan War. We may recall the story, not mentioned in Homer, but reported by Proclus in his summary of the *Cypria,* where Odysseus himself tried to avoid joining the expedition against Troy by feigning madness. The manner of Orsilochus's murder recalls Meriones's expertise in ambush. Of course, nocturnal ambush also plays a role in Odysseus's clever tale to coax a warm cloak out of Eumaeus (14.468–506). On a chilly night in Troy while lying in ambush, Odysseus managed to furnish the Cretan stranger with a cloak by means of a ruse. Eumaeus gets the point of the story and offers a blanket and cloak to the disguised Odysseus to ward off the cold night air. The piquancy of the ploy is enhanced if we remember that, in the remarkably similar setting of the Doloneia, Odysseus alone of the heroes goes forth without a cloak but acquires at the end the wolf pelt of Dolon. In his initial conversation with Penelope, Odysseus retains his Cretan disguise but at the same time suppresses much that might have appeared seamy in his earlier false tales. At the same time, he elevates himself to the closest family relation to the Cretan king—Idomeneus.

Outstanding skill in archery has played no part in Odysseus's Cretan tales, although Cretans were generally known as good bowmen in antiquity. But the hero of the *Odyssey* has an intriguing relationship to the expert archer of the *Iliad*. For Meriones's prize for his wonderful exhibition shot is none other than ten *double axes*. Double axes, of course, form a crucial element in Odysseus's own master shot and the climax of the *Odyssey*. Now, it is well known that in the *Iliad* Odysseus does not appear as a bowman. But in the passage from the Doloneia that prompted these reflections, Odysseus borrows not only the helmet but also a bow from the same Meriones. Only in the *Odyssey* do we learn why Odysseus came to Troy without his bow. Its history too will require further investigation, but, in any case, archery provides yet another link between Meriones and Odysseus.

There is a modern critic who seems to suspect something of the complex interconnections between Odysseus and the figure of Meriones. In his book on the Doloneia, Shewan cryptically remarks that Eumaeus, upon hearing the disguised Odysseus's tale, must have thought to himself: "You must be Meriones himself!" Unfortunately, Shewan has nothing more to say on the subject. There is, however, an interesting piece of ancient testimony in an unlikely place connecting Odysseus and Meriones . . . and helmets (Plutarch, *Life of Marcellus* 20.3):

> There is a city of Sicily, called Engyium, not large but very ancient, and famous for the appearance there of goddesses, who are called Mothers. The temple is said to have been built by the Cretans, and certain spears were shown there, and bronze helmets; one of these bore the name of Meriones, and others that of Ulysses (that is, Odysseus), who had consecrated them to the goddesses.
>
> (Translated by B. Perrin)

Plutarch's statement suggests that the connection between Odysseus and Meriones is not purely "literary," but that it finds a reflection in the traditional lore embodied in cult. I must leave to others the exploration of these "far reaches of mythology." The evidence, however allusive, is sufficient to show that the intricate cluster of associations linking Meriones and Odysseus is no mere coincidence. This, in turn, implies that, on the literary level, the relationship between the *Odyssey*, the Doloneia, and the *Iliad* may be far more complex than is generally recognized.

But let us return to the question of the boar's-tusk helmet from which we began. The Autolycan inheritance of Odysseus, of which the helmet is an emblem, seems to surface most clearly in Odysseus's lying tales. The "thievery and equivocal oath" of the grandfather are not transmitted to his grandson without change. Rather, they are transmuted into a gift for lies and deceptive speech: Cretan tales. And this is the very talent for which Athena praises her favorite: "deceptive and thievish tales, which are dear to you from the bottom of your heart" (ἀπατάων/μύθων τε κλοπίων, οἵ τοι πεδόθεν φίλοι εἰσιν, 13.294–95). By means of this modification, the helmet of Autolycus fits the head of Odysseus.

K*leos* and Its Ironies
in the *Odyssey*

Charles Segal

Heroic glory, ϰλέος [*kleos*], occupies a central place not only in Greek epic, but in the entire Indo-European epic tradition. In the *Iliad* a warrior's kleos is more important than life itself, as Achilles's ultimate choice makes clear. In a shame-culture, like that of the society depicted in Homer, where esteem depends on how one is viewed and talked of by one's peers, kleos is fundamental as a measure of one's value to others and to oneself. Both of the Homeric poems, however, while based on this value-system, also comment on it and even explore its limits. Achilles does this explicitly in *Iliad* 9. The *Odyssey* too, rather more indirectly, also questions heroic values and the concept of kleos which lies at its center. The complexities and ironies in the *Odyssey*'s view of kleos form the subject of this paper.

The *Odyssey* is remarkable for its self-consciousness about the social function of heroic poetry, the contexts in which such poetry is performed, and the rapport between the bard and his hearers. On three occasions situations of bardic recitation are described in detail: the song of Phemius in book 1, the songs of Demodocus in book 8, and the *apologoi* recited by Odysseus himself, especially in book 11. When he introduces the disguised Odysseus into the palace, Eumaeus also compares his story-telling skill to that of a bard (17.518–21). These passages help relate the values of heroic kleos directly to the bardic tradition that keeps it alive: they show that tradition operating before our eyes (and in our ears) in the songs about great deeds of the past which poets sing and men "hear" from generation to generation.

From *L'Antiquité Classique* 52 (1983). © 1983 by the University of Brussels.

In the first two of these situations, the songs of Phemius and De-modocus, a curious reversal takes place: instead of the *terpsis,* the joy or delight which song should bring, these songs bring grief, pain, and tears (1.336–52; 8:62ff.; 11.333–69). When Odysseus tells his tale, moreover, he is compared explicitly to a bard by King Alcinoos (11.368). Shortly before, the effects of his song were remarked in third-person narrative: he held everyone in silence, just like Phemius in book 1 (11.333 = 1.339). His song, like Phemius's, casts a spell or enchantment (κηληθμῷ, 11.334; cf. θελκτήρια, 1.337). Alcinoos compliments him not only on his skill in general (ἐπισταμένως, 11.368), but also specifically on the beauty of his verbal expression as well as on the wisdom or good sense of its contents (11.367: σοι δ᾽ ἔπι μὲν μορφὴ ἐπέων, ἔνι δὲ φρένες ἐσθλαί). Now, a hero or bard may sing of the "glorious deeds of men," the κλέα ἀνδρῶν, as Achilles does in *Illiad* 9 or Demodocus in *Odyssey,* 8.73. But what elicits Alcinoos's praise here (as more naturally Arete's in 11.336–41) is a tale about women. This interruption of Odysseus's narrative, the only one which occurs, follows immediately upon the "Catalogue of Heroines."

This inversion in the hero's "bardic" role as a singer of the κλέα ἀνδρῶν takes on a broader significance in the light of the passage in which Odysseus announces his heroic identity at the beginning of his tale:

εἴμ᾽ Ὀδυσεὺς Λαερτιάδης, ὃς πᾶσι, δόλοισιν
ἀνθρώποισι μέλω, και μεν κλέος οὐρανόν ἵκει.

["I am Odysseus son of Laertes, known before all men
for the study of crafty designs, and my fame goes up to the
    heavens."]

(9.19–20)

These lines have several noteworthy features. First, with one partial ex-ception, to be discussed later, this is the only place in the *Odyssey* where a character speaks of his own kleos. It is also the only place in Homer where μέλω, common in the third person in this sense, "be a concern to," occurs in the first person. The closest parallel in this association of μέλει with enduring fame or kleos is Circe's brief allusion to the Argo as πᾶσι μέλουσα (12.70), a usage appropriate to a ship famed in legend and probably already celebrated in epic song. In using the verb in the first person here in book 9, Odysseus calls attention to the fact that he is, in a sense, singing a kleos which normally would be recited *about* him in the third person.

The Homeric hero is generally unreticent about his own achievements. His kleos, however, the fame which is "heard" among men (cf. *Iliad*, 2.486), lives in the mouths of the bard, not of the hero himself. As Walter Marg puts it [in *Homer über die Dichtung*], "Ruhm, weiter und dauernder, über den Tod hinaus, ist das grosse Verlangen der homerischen Helden. Ihn gibt vor allem der Sänger, der die Kunde befestigt und weiterträgt [Fame, more widespread and more lasting, even beyond death, is the great demand of the Homeric hero. It is conferred chiefly by the bard, who celebrates and perpetuates the information.]" This kleos is for others to sing, for "strangers to carry around the wide world," as Penelope says (19.333), or to spread "wide over Greece and the midlands of Argos" (1.344 = 4.726 = 4.816), or for gods to embody in "graceful song among men who live on the earth" (24.196; cf. *Iliad*, 6.357f.). As the parallels in the Indic epic tradition suggest, κλέος ἄφθιτον is not merely a creation of men, but something akin to the eternal elements of the world, possessed of an objective existence in the lives of societies and their traditions.

In the *Iliad* it is rare for a hero to speak of "my glory," ἐμὸν κλέος, in the first person. A hero may talk of "winning *kleos* for myself," as Hector does when he boasts of his martial prowess:

> οὐδέ με θυμὸς ἄνωγεν, ἐπεὶ μάθον ἔμμεναι ἐσθλὸς
> αἰεὶ καὶ πρώτοισι μετὰ Τρώεσσι μάχεσθαι,
> ἀρνύμενος πατρός τε μέγα κλέος ἠδ᾽ ἐμὸν αὐτοῦ.

["and the spirit will not let me, since I have learned to be
   valiant
and to fight always among the foremost ranks of the
   Trojans,
winning for my own self great glory, and for my
   father."]

(*Iliad*, 6.444–46)

Even here kleos is something to be won and is closely associated with the father as well as the individual hero.

Parallels to Odysseus's phrasing occur at two moments of special heroic intensity in the *Iliad*. Achilles in 9.412–16 contrasts the κλέος ἄφθιτον that he will win if he fights at Troy with long life and loss of kleos (ὤλετό μοι κλέος ἐσθλόν, 9.415). Even here, where ἐμόν is not actually used, the hero's kleos is not something achieved and final. Quite the contrary, it seems remote and beyond his direct control. Hector's challenge to the Greek army in *Iliad* 7 offers a closer parallel: his opponent will die, Hector boasts, "but my *kleos* will not perish" (*Iliad*, 7.91: τὸ δ᾽ ἐμὸν κλέος οὔ ποτ᾽ ὀλεῖται). Here, too, as in *Iliad*, 6.446 above, the hero is in the process of creating that kleos. Similarly, Achilles in *Iliad*, 9.415 stands at a moment of crucial decision which will determine whether or not that kleos will exist in the future.

The situation of Odysseus at 9.19–20 is very different. He is not involved in action or decision. He is, in fact, far from the heroic world, safe among the soft, luxury-loving Phaeacians. He is not creating that kleos by fighting, but rather re-creating it by the "Ich-Erzählung" of the long, bard-like narrative which is to occupy the next four books. Both hero and bard, he is in the unique position of being the singer of his own kleos. His kleos, in other words, gains both a subjective and an objective aspect. The interlude in book 11 makes this double function explicit.

The anomalous position of Odysseus as the reciter of his own kleos, in other words, brings together two aspects of kleos which are usually kept separate. First, as Nagy has recently suggested, kleos is "the formal word which the Singer himself (*aoidos*) used to designate the songs which he sang in praise of gods and men, or, by extension, the songs which people learned to sing from him." Second, kleos is also the objectification of the hero's personal survival in epic song, the "imperishable fame" which lives among men and keeps alive the hero's name. Thus, as Nagy points out, the usual translation of kleos as "fame" is inadequate, for "fame" indicates only "the consequences rather than the full semantic range," whereas in fact the relation between the actual "fame" of the hero and the medium which preserves that "fame" is more complex: "The actions of gods and heroes gain fame through the medium of the Singer, and the Singer calls his medium kleos."

By removing Odysseus far from the locus of his great heroic achievements at Troy and even from the adventures of the more recent past, the poet views kleos retrospectively. It is already fixed as part of an heroic tradition. That tradition can itself be held up for reflection, examination, criticism. Odysseus's encounters with the Cyclops and with Scylla, for example, reveal the inappropriateness of the traditional heroic response of straightforward battle in this strange world of fabulous monsters (9.299–306); 12:226–33).

Aware of the increasing discrepancies between the heroic world of the epic cycle and the contemporary world of his audience, the poet of the *Odyssey* calls attention to the fact that the glory of heroic deeds exists only through song: it is truly kleos in the sense of the tales that men know by hearsay (κλέος οἶον ἀκούομεν, *Iliad*, 2.486). The great deeds of the past, in other words, are now especially designated as a part of heroic song qua song. Their "objective" existence as unquestioned events which the audience accepts when it is under the "spell" of the poet's magic (*thelxis, kēlēthmos*) yields momentarily to an awareness of the form which makes possible that spell. The magic of the singer is necessary to call these deeds into being and give them their life. The "message" appears, for a moment, as the creation of its "medium." Hesiod, looking at the epic tradition from a certain distance, can even go so far as to suggest that the poet's Muses can speak falsehood that resembles "truth":

> ἴδμεν ψεύδεα πολλὰ λέγειν ἐτύμοισιν ὁμοῖα,
> ἴδμεν δ᾽, εὖτ᾽ ἐθέλωμεν, ἀληθέα γηρύσασθαι.
> (*Thesiod*)

Odysseus, able to tell tales with the skill of a bard in book 11, can also tell stories which make falsehood seem like truth after the manner of Hesiod's Muses: ἴσκε ψεύδεα πολλὰ λέγων ἐτύμοισιν ὁμοῖα [He knew how to say many false things that were like true sayings] (19.203).

The *Iliad* offers a few brief glimpses of kleos self-consciously denoted as a creation of bardic tradition. Helen reflects upon the fame in song (ἀοίδιμοι) that she and Paris will have in the songs of men of later time (*Iliad*, 6.356–58). Achilles, at a crucial point for his own kleos, sings the κλέα ἀνδρῶν (*Iliad*, 9.189). On the other hand a later poet like Ibycus is quite overt about the distinction and the interdependence between the objective kleos of heroes which the poet transmits and the personal "fame" which the medium confers.

II

Odysseus's formulation of his kleos in book 9, lines 19–20 has yet another anomaly. His kleos derives not from heroic deeds achieved in the forefront of the battle, like Hector's in *Iliad* 6.446, but from their opposite, *doloi*. A syntactical ambiguity accompanies the ambiguity of the kleos:

> εἴμ᾽ Ὀδυσεὺς Λαερτιάδης, ὃς πᾶσι δόλοισιν
> ἀνθρώποισι μέλω, καί μευ κλέος οὐρανὸν ἵκει.

["I am Odysseus son of Laertes, known before all men
for the study of crafty designs, and my fame goes up to the
heavens."]

(9.19–20)

Πᾶσι is so placed that it can go either with ἀνθρώποισι or with δόλοις.
Odysseus's kleos can be a universal fame ("all men"), or a fame won for
the thoroughness of his trickery, the totality of his immersion in unheroic
guile ("all ruses").

Odysseus's description of himself here is to be connected with the
sinister side of himself contained in his name: identity as "the man of
pains" (ὀδύναι) or the man "doomed to odium" (ὀδύσ(σ)ομαι; cf. 1.62;
5.340, 423; 19.275, 406–9). Odysseus's very name, as Dimock, Austin,
and others have pointed out, so deliberately concealed or revealed, associates him with the ambiguous practices of trickery and his descent
from the trickster Autolycus. That ambiguity is perhaps also present in
μέλω, whose unique Homeric occurrence in the first person I have already
noted. Μέλω can mean "I am a concern to men in song," but also "I
am a care to men," i.e., a "worry," "concern," or "problem" to men in
a more negative sense (cf. 5.6).

Odysseus's representation of himself as an ambiguous hero of dolos
is all the more striking in the light of Penelope's very different view of
him and his kleos at the end of book 4. She fears the loss of her noble
and courageous husband whom she describes as

παντοίης ἀρετῇσι κεκασμένον ἐν Δαναοῖσιν
ἐσθλόν, τοῦ κλέος εὐρὺ καθ᾽ Ἑλλάδα καὶ μέσον Ἄργος.

[and who among the Danaans surpassed in all virtues,
and great, whose fame goes wide through Hellas and
midmost Argos.]

(4.725f. = 4.815f.)

Viewing Odysseus nostalgically from the needy perspective of Ithaca,
Penelope endows him with the traditional heroic aretai and the traditional
wide-spreading kleos. Odysseus himself, fighting his way out of the
strange fairyland world of his sea travels, sojourning among the unwarlike
Phaeacians, has come to experience and value a very different aspect of
himself. Encounters with monsters like Polyphemus, soon to be described, have taught him the futility of the Danaan aretai that Penelope
praises and the emptiness of the kleos that spreads far and wide over

Hellas and the midst of Argos. Here he needs a larger, more universal, more convertible form of kleos. He must also exercise skills which have an ambiguous value among the warriors at Troy.

Odysseus's formula here, *κλέος οὐρανὸν ἵκει*, reflects another peculiarity of his kleos. Fame being as central as it is to both epics, one would expect this formula to be of frequent occurrence. In fact it occurs only once in the *Iliad*, significantly of a solid, durable, but not otherwise particularly famous object, Nestor's shield (*Iliad*, 8.192). It occurs only three times in the *Odyssey*, here in 9.20 and also in 8.74 and 19.108. It is striking that neither of the other two instances describes the martial glory of a traditional epic hero. *Odyssey*, 8.73f. do not refer to a warrior at all, but to song: the muse inspires Demodocus to sing a "lay whose *kleos* mounts to the broad heavens."

The other occurrence is more striking still. It describes Penelope whom Odysseus, disguised as a beggar, addresses for the first time in the darkened halls of his palace:

> ἦ γάρ σευ κλέος οὐρανὸν εὐρὺν ἱκάνει,
> ὥς τέ τευ ἦ βασιλῆος ἀμύμονος.

["your fame goes up into the wide heaven,
as of some king who, as a blameless man and god-fearing."]
(19.108–9)

One of several "reverse similes" applied to Penelope, this one too places heroic kleos in a new and unfamiliar light. A noble queen keeping her fidelity to her absent lord in the palace has kleos as well as a warrior facing his enemies on the open field of battle. Though nothing overt is said, a situation is created in which each recognizes and begins to revivify the obscured kleos of the other. Here the threatened queen, beset by dangers, approaching desperation, lacking a firm protector in her house, receives this formula of heroic honor from the king in the guise of a starving, homeless beggar. Not only is he without kleos at this point, but he is even without name. He explicitly asks Penelope not to inquire about his lineage or his homeland, for that would fill him with grief and painful memory:

> μηδὲ μοι ἐξερέεινε γένος καὶ πατρίδα γαῖαν,
> μή μοι μᾶλλον θυμὸν ἐνιπλήσῃς ὀδυνάων
> μνησαμένῳ· μάλα δ᾽ εἰμὶ πολύστονος.

["but do not ask who I am, the name of my country,
for fear you may increase in my heart its burden of sorrow
as I think back; I am very full of grief."]

(19.116–18)

The situation utterly reverses heroic practice. The traditional warrior who
guards his kleos as his most precious possession proudly boasts his name,
his race, his origins, and his native land, as for instance Glaukos does in
his encounter with Diomedes in *Iliad,* 6.150ff. Penelope makes the appropriate reply; here, for the only time in the poem besides 9.19f., a
character speaks of kleos in the first person. Repeating lines which she
had used to the suitor Eurymachos in the previous book, she says that
her kleos would be greater only if Odysseus should return and care for
her:

εἰ κεῖνός γ᾽ ἐλθὼν τὸν ἐμὸν βίον ἀμφιπολεύοι,
μεῖζόν κε κλέος εἴη ἐμὸν καὶ κάλλιον οὕτω.

["If he were to come back to me and take care of my life,
    then
my reputation would be more great and splendid."]

(19.127f. = 18.254f.)

Now, she continues, instead of the kleos which should give joy, she has
only ἄχος, grief (19.129 = 18.256, νῦν δ᾽ ἄχομαι). In the speech in
book 18 she spoke mournfully of the difficulty of Odysseus's return and
complained of the Suitors' behavior, but here she tells the story of her
web (19.137–56). Her tale reveals that her kleos, like Odysseus's in 9.19f.,
has its basis in doloi; and in fact she precedes her account of "weaving"
the shroud with her "weaving of guile" (19.137): ἐγὼ δὲ δόλους τολυ-
πεύω.

This combination of dolos and the highest heroic kleos again points
up the paradoxes and contradictions in Odysseus's "heroism." A woman
can be expected to use doloi for her kleos, but a hero should win his
kleos in fair fight on the battlefield. Yet for the woman too dolos is
ambiguous: it can lead to the exact opposite of kleos, namely "shame"
and "disgrace," αἰσχύνη or αἶσχος. The notorious example of this latter
is Clytaemnestra, whose "guileful" planning (δολόμητις, 11.422) and
fashioning of guile (δόλον ἤρτυε, 11.439) "poured down shame (αἶσχος)
on herself and on all women after her" (11.433f.). Both Penelope and
Odysseus tread a fine line where dolos leads to "glory," not "shame." In

this respect, as in so many others, Odysseus and Penelope complement and parallel one another.

This complementation of dolos and kleos for them both is especially clear in the second Nekyia. Amphimedon tells Agamemnon the full account of Penelope's "guile" (note dolos in 24.128 and 141; cf. πολυκέρδειαι, 24.167). He at once contrasts her with Clytaemnestra (24.196–202). He praises her "great *arete*" and "good sense," and declares that "the glory of her *arete* will never perish" (τῷ οἱ κλέος οὔ ποτ᾽ ὀλεῖται / ἧς ἀρετῆς, 196f.). The gods will make her a subject of "lovely song" (ἀοιδὴν χαρίεσσαν), whereas Clytaemnestra will be a subject of "hateful song" and bring ill-fame to women (στυγερὴ ἀοιδή; χαλεπὴν φῆμιν, 200, 201). Penelope can use dolos, but still win the kleos and arete which are diametrically opposite to Clytaemnestra's αἶσχος and στυγερὴ ἀοιδή. Odysseus, on the other hand, master of disguise and trickery, nevertheless fights an heroic battle of sorts (24.178–90), whereas lordly Agamemnon dies "a most pitiable death" (11.412), unable even to get his hands on the heroic weapon (11.423–25). This last scene contrasts with the heroic exertion of Odysseus's son at the crucial moment of battle:

αὐτὰρ ἐγὼ ποτὶ γαίῃ χεῖρας ἀείρων
βάλλον ἀποθνῄσκων περὶ φασγάνῳ

["but I lifted my hands and with them beat on
the ground as I died upon the sword."]
(11.423f.)

ἀμφὶ δὲ χεῖρα φίλην βάλεν ἔγχεϊ.

["and closed his own hand over his spear."]
(21.433)

Agamemnon's heroism cannot cope with a woman's doloi; Odysseus, meeting Penelope on her own ground, can enlist their separate doloi jointly in the reestablishment, rather than the destruction, of their house and their kleos. At the crucial transition between fairyland and Ithaca in his landing on Scheria Odysseus had praised the "good fame" which husband and wife enjoy when they live together in "harmony of spirit," *homophrosynē* (6.180–85): μάλιστα δέ τ᾽ ἔκλυον αὐτοί, (6.185). That remote prayer for Nausicaa and her prospective husband now becomes relevant for Penelope and himself, fulfilled in the reaffirmed kleos of his Ithacan wife.

The poem defines heroism through a series of symmetries and inversions: Odyssean doloi contrasts with Agamemnon's kleos, the success of the one with the failure of the other. The house-destroying dolos of Clytaemnestra also contrasts with the house-preserving dolos of Penelope, as *aischos* contrasts with kleos. Simultaneously the kleos of Odysseus, paradoxically achieved through dolos, parallels the kleos of Penelope: she is a woman who weaves guile (19.137), but, woman though she is, still gains the kleos usually reserved for male heroes. He, a hero of the Trojan war, possessing the masculine kleos of the warrior, wins that kleos through dolos and, in this poem, through a deed executed in the interior space of the house, the realm usually associated with women. The Iliadic warrior at once announces his name to his antagonist; Odysseus wins his major triumphs by circumspectly (and often unheroically) hiding his name.

III

Odysseus's "fame" which "reaches to the heavens" in 9.20 recurs later in that same book in an exploit which contains one of his most brilliant doloi and forms one of the most important parts of his kleos. In 9.251ff. he has his first face-to-face encounter with the monstrous Cyclops. He addresses him, for the first time, as follows:

'Ημεῖς τοι Τροίηθεν ἀποπλαγχθέντες Ἀχαιοὶ
παντοίοις ἀνέμοισιν ὑπὲρ μέγα λαῖτμα θαλάσσης,
οἴκαδε ἱέμενοι, ἄλλην ὁδὸν ἄλλα κέλευθα
ἤλθομεν· οὕτω που Ζεὺς ἤθελε μητίσασθαι.
λαοὶ δ᾽ Ἀτρεΐδεω Ἀγαμέμνονος εὐχόμεθ᾽ εἶναι,
τοῦ δὴ νῦν γε μέγιστον ὑπουράνιον κλέος ἐστίν·
τόσσην γὰρ διέπερσε πόλιν καὶ ἀπώλεσε λαοὺς
πολλούς.

["We are Achaians coming from Troy, beaten off our true
    course
by winds from every direction across the great gulf of the
    open
sea, making for home, by the wrong way, on the wrong
    courses.
So we have come. So it has pleased Zeus to arrange it.
We claim we are of the following of the son of Atreus,
Agamemnon, whose fame now is the greatest thing under
    heaven,

such a city was that he sacked and destroyed so many
people."]

(9.259–66)

Odysseus here presents himself in terms both of his helpless wanderings
on the vast sea and of the heroic glory of his Trojan exploits, the capture
and destruction of a great city which constitute the "greatest *kleos* under
the heavens" of his leader (264f.). That same configuration, wanderings
and capturing Troy, introduces Odysseus as the hero of the poem in its
very first lines:

Ἄνδρα μοι ἔννεπε, μοῦσα, πολύτροπον, ὃς μάλα πολλὰ
πλάγχθη, ἐπεὶ Τροίης ἱερὸν πτολίεθρον ἔπερσε·

[Tell me, Muse, of the man of many ways, who was driven
far journeys, after he had sacked Troy's sacred citadel.]

(1.1f.)

Far from Troy and Trojan heroism, however, this μέγιστον ὑπούρανιον
κλέος has little meaning. It certainly makes little impression on the Cyclops, who "with pitiless spirit" dismisses his appeal for suppliant rights
(9.272–80). Odysseus replies with δολίοις ἐπέεσιν (9.282): one may hark
back proudly to martial deeds at Troy, but in this post-Trojan world the
hero will have to achieve kleos by new means.

The narrative context of the wide kleos of 9.264 contains another
irony. "The greatest distance possible," Norman Austin remarks à pro-
pos of the spatial field of Homer's world, "Homer expresses in the pro-
portion: Agamemnon's glory is as widely dispersed beneath the sky as
the city was great which he destroyed." Odysseus borrows from his
leader at Troy a kleos which embraces the sky and the earth. But Odysseus speaks of the great void of the sea (μέγα λαῖτμα θαλάσσης, 260)
and of this vast kleos under the heavens at the point when he is trapped
in a cave which, though "wide" (9.237), is nevertheless a dark and rather
crowded (219–23) enclosure (cf. μυχὸν ἄντρου, 236). He is dwarfed by
the giant who towers above him (cf. 9.257) and uses his massive strength
to seal that enclosure with a rock that not even twenty-two wagons could
budge (9.240–43). The rock both makes the enclosure definitive and
renders futile traditional heroic battle with the sword (9.299–305).

There is one further irony. Odysseus invokes with pride and confidence the kleos of a leader whose death, as he will relate in the Nekyia
of book 11, was anything but glorious (11.406–34). Agamemnon illus-

trates the failure and inadequacy of the traditional kleos in this world. Citing him, Odysseus will also find an alternative.

To defeat the Cyclops, Odysseus has to resort to the extreme form of dolos, temporarily negating his personal identity and becoming οὖτις-μῆτις, "No Man" (9.366), which is also the μῆτις of his guile or dolos. The pun associates the abandonment of heroic identity with the guile upon which he has increasingly to rely in this strange world. Later he resumes the traditional heroic stance and boasts like an Iliadic warrior over a defeated enemy. He makes the mistake here of addressing the Cyclops "with insults" (κερτομίοισι, 9.474) rather than with "guile" (9.282). The result is disastrous (9.504f.): in possession of his enemy's name, the Cyclops can call down the curse of Poseidon against him (9.503f.; cf. 504f.).

In this passage Odysseus assumes the heroic, warrior epithet, "sacker of cities," πτολιπόρθιον. He thereby identifies himself with the Iliadic kleos of his leader in whose name he introduced himself to the Cyclops in 9.265, διέπερσε πόλιν. May one speculate that by the time Odysseus has reached Alcinoos's court he is more aware of the incongruity of that martial epithet in this marine realm? By now he has learned to regard himself less as a "sacker of cities" than as a man of guile and tricks:

εἴμ᾽ Ὀδυσεὺς Λαερτιάδης, ὃς πᾶσι δόλοισιν
ἀνθρώποισι μέλω, καί μευ κλέος οὐρανὸν ἵκει.

["I am Odysseus son of Laertes, known before all men
for the study of crafty designs, and my fame goes up to the
    heavens."]

(9.19f.)

In achieving the final restoration of his heroic status too, Odysseus will need doloi more than the martial prowess of a "sacker of cities."

The converse of Odysseus's inappropriately heroic address to the Cyclops occurs in the next book. Landing on another unknown island, Odysseus confesses his disorientation (10.189–97): he does not know the celestial coordinates of east and west, sunrise and sunset, and finds himself at a loss for his usual *mētis*:

ἀλλά φραζώμεθα θᾶσσον,
εἴ τις ἔτ᾽ ἔσται μῆτις. ἐγὼ δ᾽ οὐκ οἴομαι εἶναι.

["let us hasten our minds and think, whether there is
any course left open to us. But I think there is none."]

(10.192f.)

At this declaration his men's spirit is broken as they remember the violence (*biē*) of the Cyclops and Laestrygonians (10.198–200), and they weep miserably (201f.). Not only is there an antithesis of mētis and biē, as acted out in the Polyphemus episode, but the absence of Odysseus's mētis, closely akin to his dolos, results in a loss of speech: his men can only "wail shrilly" and lament (10.201f.): κλαῖον δὲ λιγέως θαλερὸν κατὰ δάκρυ χέοντες. "Guileful words," δόλια ἔπεα, are the saving device of Odysseus's mētis against brute force (9.282). Shortly before, his "honeyed words" of encouragement (μειλίχια ἔπεα, 10.173) kept his men from grieving about death (10.172–78). Now, in the absence of his mētis, words give way to inarticulate and helpless grief (ἀλλ᾽ οὐ γάρ τις πρῆξις ἐγίγνετο μυρομένοισιν, 10.202). Soon afterwards, these dispirited companions, lacking the guidance of Odyssean mētis, lose their human voice (*phōnē*, 10.239) and in their bestial transformation by Circe are penned up "wailing" (κλαίοντες, 10.241).

IV

In 9.19f., as we have seen, Odysseus's formal declaration of his heroic identity has associations with the bardic view of kleos as something past and definitively formed: he sings as his own a kleos which ought to come from another's mouth. In book 11 Odysseus actually performs as a bard who skilfully sings a warrior's deeds. In the Phaeacian perspective of aesthetic distance, martial exploits and painful suffering appear only as art. But when Odysseus faces his great deed of restoring order on Ithaca and regaining name and kingdom, he sets up just the reverse relation of art and action. No longer the soldier doing the work of a bard, but a beggar in disguise, he elicits from his regal weapon the sound which is music to the warrior's ears. Holding the great bow, finally, in his hands, he handles it as a poet handles a lyre:

ὡς ὅτ᾽ ἀνὴρ φόρμιγγος ἐπιστάμενος καὶ ἀοιδῆς
ῥηϊδίως ἐτάνυσσε νέῳ περὶ κόλλοπι χορδήν,
ἅψας ἀμφοτέρωθεν ἐϋστρεφὲς ἔντερον οἰός,
ὡς ἄρ᾽ ἄτερ σπουδῆς τάνυσεν μέγα τόξον Ὀδυσσεύς.
δεξιτερῇ δ᾽ ἄρα χειρὶ λαβὼν πειρήσατο νευρῆς·
ἡ δ᾽ ὑπὸ καλὸν ἄεισε, χελιδόνι εἰκέλη αὐδήν.

[as when a man, who well understands the lyre and singing,
easily, holding it on either side, pulls the strongly twisted
cord of sheep's gut, so as to slip it over a new peg,

so, without any strain, Odysseus strung the great bow.
Then plucking it in his right hand he tested the bowstring,
and it gave him back an excellent sound like the voice of a
    swallow.]

(21.406–11)

Tried by Odysseus, the bow "sings beautifully" like a swallow—or, as
the verb ἄεισε also suggests, like a bard (21.410f.). The order, aesthetic
and social, implied by song now begins once more to approximate the
moral and political order reestablished by the return of the King. Disorder
in Mycenae, we recall, included the banishment of the bard whom Agamemnon left to guard his queen (3.267–72).

Among the Phaeacians Odysseus could recreate his heroic past and
its kleos only in song. Here on Ithaca he is a warrior who brings back
to the palace the joy and rightful celebration of heroic deeds which earlier
could only be evoked by bards whose tales made the listeners weep. The
joyful songs of Phemius and of Demodocus on Scheria caused private
grief to Penelope and Odysseus, but gave public "joy" (τέρψις) to the
rest of the audience (cf. 1.342, 347; 8.91f., 536–43; 9.3–15). The "song"
of the bow gives public "grief" (ἄχος) to the audience at large (21.412,
supra), but private "rejoicing" to Odysseus (21.414): γήθησέν τ' ἄρ'
ἔπειτα πολύτλας δῖος Ὀδυσσεύς. This inversion of joy and grief now
refers not merely to the quiet, interior bardic situation when Odysseus
was isolated in the house of strangers, but also to the heroic situation on
the battlefield, where the bow brings a living kleos to one and "grief"
(πένθος) to the other in actual deeds, not their reflection in song. We
may compare the wounding of Menelaus in *Iliad*, 4.196–97 = 206–7:

> ὅν τις ὀιστεύσας ἔβαλεν τόξων ἐῢ εἰδώς,
> Τρώων ἢ Λυκίων, τῷ μὲν κλέος, ἄμμι δὲ πένθος.

["the warlike son of
Atreus, whom someone skilled in the bow's use shot with
    an arrow,
Trojan or Lykian: glory to him, but to us a sorrow."]

When Odysseus sang like a bard on Scheria, heroic kleos was a fossilized
vestige in the amber of the Phaeacians' unheroic hedonism (cf. 8.246–
55). In this setting a heroic declaration of kleos, like that of 9.19–20 or
like the reaction to a taunt about a more trivial kleos in an athletic, not
a martial, competition (8.152–57), could appear only as incongruous
(8.146–47). Now, at the brink of heroic battle once more, the hero uses

a bardic metaphor not merely to state in words, but to enact in deeds what it meant to win kleos at Troy.

V

This perspective on heroic song also casts fresh light on the episode of the Sirens. They are described in the vocabulary of the bard: their song casts a spell (θέλγουσι, 12.40; λιγυρῇ θέλγουσιν ἀοιδῇ, 12.44), like that of Phemius (θελκτήρια, 1.337; cf. 11.334), a vocabulary which links them with the ambiguous and seductive magic (also called *thelxis*) of Circe (10.291, 317). Their power depends emphatically on hearing (12.41, 48; 49, 52, 185, 187, 193, 198). Their "voice" is itself a "song" (*aoidē*, 12.44, 183, 198) which is "clear-sounding" (λιγυρή, 12.44, 183) or "honey-voiced" (μελίγηρυς, 187; hence the homeopathic magic of the "honey-sweet" wax, μελιηδής, 12.49, of the antidote). It also brings the "joy" or "delight," τέρψις, associated with bardic song (τερπόμενος, 12.52; τερψάμενος, 12.188; cf. 1.342, 347). The song's material is the epic tradition, the efforts at Troy as well as "what passes on the wide-nurturing earth" (12.189–91).

The rendering of the heroic tradition which the Sirens practise, how-ever, is akin, in a certain way, to the bardic song of Scheria: it shows heroic adventure as something frozen and crystallized into lifeless, static form, something dead and past, a subject for song and nothing more. For this reason, perhaps, they are the first adventure of Odysseus after Hades (12.39, Σειρῆνας μὲν πρῶτον ἀφίξεαι). Thus they stand in close proximity to that dead world of purely retrospective heroism. Yet when Odysseus had related his adventure among the dead—with the Siren-like "spell" and the art of a bard, to be sure (11.334, 368)—those shades were still a living part of his past, directly related to his *nostos* (cf. 11.100, 196). What he hears in the Underworld stirs grief or arouses indignation (11.435–39, 465f.) and thus reinforces that longing for mother, father, and wife which is essential to his return (cf. 11.152–334). What the Sirens sing is remote from any experience. The magical charm of their sweet voice on the windless sea is epic kleos in the abstract, lovely, but somehow dehumanized (cf. the vast generality of ὅσσα γένηται ἐπὶ χθονὶ πουλυβοτείρῃ, 12.191).

As the past of which the Sirens sing has the deathly vacuity of what is long dead and without flesh (cf. 12.45f.), so they themselves are char-acterized by motionlessness. As Odysseus and his men draw near, a wind-less calm forces them to take to the oars (12.167–72). These Sirens, unlike their later descendants in Greek art, do not fly, but "sit" (ἥμεναι ἐν λειμῶνι, 12.45) and ask Odysseus to "stop the ship" (νῆα κατάστησον, 12.185) in order to hear their voice. They claim that no one "has ever yet passed by (παρήλασε) in black ship before hearing the honey-voiced speech from our mouths" (12.186f.). Escape from them, therefore, consists in keeping active, moving, passing by (παρὲξ ἐλάαν, 12.47; παρήλασαν, 12.197).

Not only do the Sirens know of the exploits at Troy, but they also address Odysseus by the heroic epithet, μέγα κῦδος Ἀχαιῶν, (12.184). This is the only place in the poem where he is so titled. This epithet occurs seven times in the *Iliad*. It has only two other occurrences in the *Odyssey*, here and the formulaic line by which Telemachus twice addresses the aged Nestor in book 3 (3.79 = 202). Well might the inexperienced youth at his first direct contact with the glories of Troy address the oldest of the Achaean warriors in these terms, terms which perhaps remind us that Nestor, more than any other Homeric character, lives in the past.

Odysseus, however, will continue his journey and effect a return to the living past and living kleos that await him on Ithaca, not at Troy. He must therefore resist the blandishment of the heroic tradition as frozen into this spell-binding, but lifeless song. What the Sirens know is too general and too remote to help him in his quest to recover Ithaca. To remain and listen to their song would be to yield to the seduction of a heroic tradition rendered in its most elegant, attractive, and deadly form, devoid of reality for the tasks that await this hero of dolos. The Nekyia and, in a different way, the lives of Nestor and Menelaus have shown this danger in lived example. The Sirens cast that danger of entrapment by the past specifically into the form of poetic song and the fascination it exercises. Were he to heed it, he too would be frozen into a sterile past, one of those rotting skeletons on the island. His task, therefore, is not to listen, but to "pass by."

Rather than preserving fame by the remembering Muse of true epic song (Muse, after all, is probably etymologically akin to "memory"), the Sirens bring forgetfulness of home and loved ones (12.42f.). Pindar told how golden "charmers" (Keledones), akin to these Sirens, perched atop a mythical temple of Apollo at Delphi and sang so sweetly that the visitors "perished there apart from wives and children, their souls suspended at their honeyed voice" (Snell, *Paean* 8.75–79). For Odysseus thus to perish obscurely on the rock to which the magic of the Sirens' song draws him would be to forget the "return" (nostos) on which in fact his kleos rests.

In this temptation of "forgetting the return" the Sirens' magical spell has affinities not only with Circe, but also with the Lotos-eaters. There too a man "forgets his return" (νόστοιο λάθηται, 9.97 and 102; cf. οἴκαδε νοστήσαντι 12.43). The victims of the Lotos, like Odysseus in book 12, have to be bound forcibly in the ship (9.99 and 12.196). The Sirens inhabit a "flowery meadow" (λειμῶν᾽ ἀνθεμόεντα, 12.159); the Lotos is a "flower-like food" (ἄνθινον εἶδαρ, 9.84).

The abode of the Sirens is characterized by death and decay. Circe describes the bones of "rotting men" near their meadow (ἀνδρῶν πυθομένων, 12.46), and Odysseus warns his men of the danger in terms of dying or avoiding death (ἵνα εἰδότες ἤ κε θάνωμεν ἤ κεν ἀλευάμενοι θάνατον καὶ κῆρα φύγοιμεν, 12.156f.). Epic song and the memory which it preserves, however, confer a victory over death. Its "imperishable fame," κλέος ἄφθιτον, is the exact antithesis of the Sirens' rot and decay. As Nagy has shown, ἄφθιτον, whose root, φθι-, "occurs frequently in the context of plants" (cf. the ἄφθιτοι ἄμπελοι of 9.133), has associations with the vital liquids or substances that overcome death:

> From the present survey of all the Greek epic nouns (except κλέος) which are described by ἄφθιτο-, we may posit a least common denominator in context: *an unfailing stream* of water, fire, semen, vegetal extract (wine). By extension, the gods representing these entities may also have the epithet ἄφθιτο-, as well as the things that they own or make.
>
> (*Comparative Studies in Greek and Indic Meter*)

True epic song counters the decay to which mortal things are subject with a kleos seen as close to the very essence of life, akin to the vital fluids that sustain the life of men and the natural world.

In the Sirens, song not only is a ghostly imitation of epic, but even becomes its own negation. This song brings death, not life. It does not go out over the broad earth among men. Those who succumb to it remain closed off from men, becalmed on a nameless sea, their bodies rotting in a flowery meadow. The Sirens know the secrets of the past, but it is a past which has no future life in the "remembering" of successive generations. Here the hero forgets his loved ones among whom his kleos might live on after his death (cf. 12.42f.). The epic bard, aided by the goddess of memory, makes the past live in the present and bridges over the void between the sunless realm of the dead and the bright world of the living, as Odysseus himself does in the Nekyia of book 11; the Sirens' song entraps the living in the putrefaction of his own hopelessly mortal remains.

Though fundamentally different in many ways, the Sirens have certain resemblances to the Harpies. "Seelenvogel," "snatchers" of the soul from life to death. In the case of Homer's Sirens, the song which should immortalize ironically bring oblivion. Where the *Odyssey* mentions these "snatchers" in relation to Odysseus, there is an interesting overlap with the Sirens, for *harpyiai* negate his kleos:

ἠδέ κε καὶ ᾧ παιδὶ μέγα κλέος ἤρατ᾽ ὀπίσσω.
νῦν δέ μιν ἀκλειῶς ἅρπυιαι ἀνηρείψαντο.

[and he would have won great fame for himself and his son
        hereafter.
But now ingloriously the stormwinds have caught and
        carried him
    away.]

(1.240f. = 14.370f.)

Closely related to this negation of Odysseus's kleos is Penelope's lament as she imagines the death not only of a husband, but also of a son, the latter also "snatched" away:

παντοίης ἀρετῆσι κεκασμένον ἐν Δαναοῖσιν
ἐσθλόν, τοῦ κλέος εὐρὺ καθ᾽ Ἑλλάδα καὶ μέσον Ἄργος.
νῦν αὖ παῖδ᾽ ἀγαπητὸν ἀνηρείψαντο θύελλαι
ἀκλέα ἐκ μεγάρων, οὐδ᾽ ὁρμηθέντος ἄκουσα.

[and who among the Danaans surpassed in all virtues,
and great, whose fame goes wide through Hellas and
midmost Argos;
and now again the stormwinds have caught away my
beloved
son, without trace, from the halls, and I never heard when
he left me.]

(4.725–28)

Such a death is analogous to the doom of the Sirens' island in book 12. The "harpies" who snatch a man away "without *kleos*" to the remote corners of the world on the winds of storm deprive him of the kleos which would be "heard" as men in a civilized community sing of a death by glorious deeds, witnessed by his comrades and commemorated by a funeral monument (1.239 = 14.369, τῷ κέν οἱ τύμβον μὲν ἐποίησαν Παναχαιοί). Lost in the obscure reaches of the wild, he would necessarily perish ἀκλειῶς, in the anonymity of nature's violence, just as the victims of the Sirens in book 12 rot in nameless heaps in a remote, mysterious ocean, reclaimed entirely by nature's elemental processes of putrefaction and decay.

The Sirens have the *terpsis* of the epic bard, but no contact with the kleos through which he conquers death. The verb which repeatedly describes the "hearing" of their song is ἀκούειν (eight times: see *supra*), never κλύειν. As their voice does not go beyond the nameless "island" (12.201) where they sit, so the "hearing" (ἀκούειν) of their song is entirely literal, not the symbolical "imperishable *kleos*" that leads from death to life. As their victims succumb to the physical decay of their physical remains and are reduced to the rotting flesh of mere body, so a purely physical blocking of the ears as the corporeal organ of hearing suffices to defeat them. Indeed Homer dwells concretely on the physical details of placing wax, a substance also used to preserve, in the ears (12.47f., 177).

Like Hesiod's Muses, the Sirens speak in the language of "knowing" (ἴδμεν ... ἴδμεν, 12.189, 191; cf. *Theogony,* 27f.), but no word of "memory" or "remembering" characterizes their song. All the basic elements of this song, then, its knowledge, pleasure, and "hearing," form a perversion of true heroic song. Whoever heeds it is caught by the fatal "spell" of empty "delight" in a purely physical "hearing" which will isolate him far from the living memory of future men. Here he will rot away obscurely, his remains indistinguishable in a heap of rotting skin and bones, not the whole forms of the active figures of heroes who breathe and move in their deeds when the epic bard awakens the κλέα ἀνδρῶν.

Seen in this perspective, the episode of the Sirens is not just another fantastic adventure of Odysseus's wanderings. Through his characteristic form of mythic image the traditional singer here finds symbolic expression for the implicit values and poetics of epic song and epic kleos.

VI

Odysseus's last words in book 21 are an ironical invocation of the nonheroic scenes of feasting and song which have occurred throughout the poem. With grim humor he suggests that it is now the time "to make merry with song and the lyre, for these are the accompaniments of the feast":

νῦν δ᾽ ὥρη καὶ δόρπον Ἀχαιοῖσιν τετυκέσθαι
ἐν φάει, αὐτὰρ ἔπειτα καὶ ἄλλως ἐψιάασθαι
μολπῇ καὶ φόρμιγγι· τὰ γάρ τ᾽ ἀναθήματα δαιτός.

["Now is the time for their dinner to be served the Achaians
in the daylight, then follow with other entertainment,
the dance and the lyre; for these things come at the end of
the feasting."]

(21.428–30)

We recall the first feast and the first song in book 1, when Odysseus
seemed hopelessly far away and the suitors controlled the palace and
forced the bard to sing (1.145–55; 1.152, cf. 21.430; 22.351f.). But now,
as the equation of lyre to bow in the similes of 405 and 411 changes from
trope to action, so the ironical invitation to feasting and song in 21.428–
30 changes to heroic combat in the military formula which close the
book:

ἀμφὶ δὲ χεῖρα φίλην βάλεν ἔγχεϊ, ἄγχι δ᾽ ἄρ᾽ αὐτοῦ
πὰρ θρόνον ἑστήκει κεκορυθμένος αἴθοπι χαλκῷ.

[and closed his own hand over his spear, and took his
position
close beside him and next the chair, all armed in bright
bronze.]

(21.433f.)

Now too the "contests" which accompanied those feasts as part of Phaeacian levity (cf. the ἄεθλοι and κλέος of 8.145–48) have higher stakes as
Odysseus opens a grimmer "contest" (22.5 = 21.92, οὗτος μὲν δὴ ἄεθ-
λος ἀάατος) and aims "at a target which no one ever yet hit" (22.6).
Odysseus no longer has to use the bard-like "charm" (thelxis) of his lies
to win his way into the palace, as he does through the tales which Eumaeus singles out when he introduces him to Penelope for the first time
(17.518–21). Making good his rightful place within the palace by a
"song" of a very different kind, Odysseus performs a final bard-like act
which both completes and supersedes all his previous skillful manipula-
tion of words.

The end of book 21 resonates in still a different register when the
great deed is really accomplished and Odysseus has purged the enemies
from his halls. Still reflecting on the practical exigencies of the situation,
Odysseus orders a bath and fresh clothes, and then gives instructions that
"the divine singer, holding the clear-sounding lyre, lead us in the playful
dance, so that one hearing it outside may say that it is a wedding"
(23.133–35). His commands are promptly obeyed: soon "the divine
singer took up the smooth lyre and stirred up in them desire for sweet

song and blameless dance" (23.143–45). Now Odysseus, not the suitors, commands song. He is indeed celebrating a wedding, in a sense, for he and Penelope, the obstacles removed, are on the verge of their reunion, the next major event in the poem (23.152–288). The motif of the wedding celebration, however, appears with a twist of bitter irony: the "Suitors" of the new "bride" are lying dead, and the festivity is the extension of the deed of killing them. The occasion for the song here in 23.133ff. contrasts both with Phemius's singing in book 1 and, more immediately, with his frightened holding of his lyre in the fear of death in 22.330ff. (22.332b = 23.133b). Phemius's song here also contrasts with the song of Demodocus in book 8. The stated aim of song in 23 is not joy (terpsis) per se, though Phemius's patronymic is Terpiades (22.330), but rather the dangerous circumstances of battle and the prospect of facing still more uneven odds (23.118–22). Not a scene of happy conviviality, but a speech about the martial virtues of valor and loyalty introduces the order that the "divine bard" play on his lyre (23.124–28). The purpose of this song, finally, is not to proclaim and perpetuate kleos, but the opposite, to *prevent* the "wide fame" of a great deed from going out into the world:

> μὴ πρόσθε κλέος εὐρὺ φόνου κατὰ ἄστυ γένηται
> ἀνδρῶν μνηστήρων.

["Let no rumor go abroad in the town that the suitors
have been murdered."]

(23.137f.)

Thus even when Odysseus accomplishes his great exploit, the usual terms of heroic kleos are inverted.

The comparison of the bow to the bard's lyre in the former passage (21.404ff.) not only introduces the long-anticipated scene of heroic combat and heroic kleos, but also brings together the two sides of Odysseus's role in the poem. By subordinating song to action (for in book 21 the bardic associations are figurative only), the similes implicitly reassert Odysseus's full return to the heroic world and to the kleos, rightfully his, that has been so problematical in the poem. He may owe that kleos to trickery, dolos, as 9.19f. suggest; yet this hero of *mētis, mēchanē*, and *polykerdeiai* is also capable of heroic battle against great odds.

At the same time an important ambiguity remains, parallel to the ambiguities of Odysseus's kleos. The slaughter of the suitors has, to be sure, some of the appurtenances of heroic battle: Athena-Mentor is there to exhort Odysseus by his valor at Troy (22.226–30). Yet this deed is hardly an heroic exploit on the Iliadic scale. From the Suitors' point of view, given a full hearing in the second Nekyia, it is guile and murder. When the slain suitor Amphimedon describes the deed, he begins with the deceit of a woman (24.125ff.), stresses the craftiness of Odysseus (24.167, *polykerdeiai*), and implies that he and his companions never had a fair chance. The heroic detail of the "lovely armor" (περικαλλέα τεύχεα, 24.165) figures only as part of the hopeless odds against which he and his companions had to contend. Like Agamemnon in book 11, he views his death not as a proud heroic end on the field of battle, but as "a wretched doom" (κακὸν τέλος, 24.124; cf. 11.412, οἰκτίστῳ θανάτῳ). As we have already seen, his speech completes the symmetries and contrasts between Odysseus and Agamemnon, Penelope and Clytaemnestra, kleos and dolos, kleos and aischos.

The peculiarities in the language of kleos which we have studied here suggest that the poet of the *Odyssey* was aware of the ambiguities attaching to his hero "of many turns." He deliberately plays off against one another different perspectives on the heroic tradition. Composing, probably, at a time when the heroic ideal is itself undergoing change and redefinition, and when, possibly, epic language is becoming more and more fluid, he uses traditional elements in new ways and refashions a hero and a style where non-heroic values and fresh social, ethical, and aesthetic currents make themselves felt.

From distanced, self-conscious, and ironic reflection on kleos, Homer returns us in the last three books of the epic, to full participation in the *making* of kleos. Odysseus's reassertion of his heroic persona and his restoration to wife, house and kingship consist precisely in this movement from singer to actor. He (re-)creates kleos in song when he recites the *apologoi* to Alcinoos's court skillfully like a professional bard, but he finally wins kleos in deeds when he makes the warrior's bow sing like the poet's lyre. Both in song and in action Odysseus's task is to restore order, domestic, civic, and cosmic. He reestablishes song and feasting as a sign of that order in his palace when the bard, spared from death by the grim warrior-king (22.330ff.), can once more play the accompaniment to joyful dancing and merriment as king and queen are about to be united (23.143–45; 22.332b = 23.133b).

With its characteristic openness toward what is new, changing, and dangerous as well as what is firm and traditional in life, the poem's last scene is not the songful feast of a reunited house in a celebratory *hieros gamos,* as one might have expected, but a scene of battle. Odysseus's last address to his son is the admonition,

> Telemachus, you yourself, stepping forth (to battle) where men fight and the best are separated out, shall learn not to shame (καταισχύνειν) the race of your fathers, for in valor and in manliness we are distinguished over the whole earth.

Is this a final realism beneath the poet's apparently happy ending? What the wily and much-enduring hero bequeathes to his son for the future is not only the visible proof of his own kleos (here defined by its opposite, non-aischos), but also the necessary experience of war.

Chronology

ca. 4000 B.C.	Dawn of Bronze Age in Crete.
ca. 3000 B.C.	Beginning of northern invasions of Greece.
ca. 2000 B.C.	Unification of Minoan power in Crete.
ca. 2000–1700 B.C.	Achaean invasion.
ca. 1600 B.C.	Destruction of Phaestos and Cnossos in Crete. Palaces rebuilt. Greek linear script replaces hieroglyphs.
ca. 1600–1400 B.C.	Strong Cretan influence in Greece. The shaft-grave dynasty at Mycenae.
ca. 1400 B.C.	Second destruction of Cretan palaces. Rapid wane of Minoan power.
ca. 1400–1200 B.C.	Great age of Mycenae. Development of Mycenaean trade in Egypt and Eastern Mediterranean. Trade with the West.
1287 B.C.	Battle of Cadesh between Egypt and Hittites; decline of both powers.
ca. 1250–1240 B.C.	Trojan War.
ca. 1180 B.C.	Troy destroyed by Mycenaeans.
ca. 1150 B.C.	Destruction of Mycenaean centers in Greece.
ca. 1100 B.C.	Successive waves of Dorian invaders penetrate Greece. "Dark Age" begins. Use of iron introduced.
ca. 800–500 B.C.	Development of the city-state from monarchy. Ionian School of lyric poetry.
776 B.C.	First Olympic Festival.
ca. 750–650 B.C.	Composition of *Iliad* and *Odyssey*.

Contributors

HAROLD BLOOM, Sterling Professor of the Humanities at Yale University, is the author of *The Anxiety of Influence, Poetry and Repression,* and many other volumes of literary criticism. His forthcoming study, *Freud: Transference and Authority,* attempts a full-scale reading of all of Freud's major writings. A MacArthur Prize Fellow, he is general editor of five series of literary criticism published by Chelsea House. During 1987–88, he served as Charles Eliot Norton Professor of Poetry at Harvard University.

H. D. F. KITTO was Professor of Greek at Bristol University. His books include *Greek Tragedy: A Literary Study, Sophocles, Dramatist and Philosopher,* and *The Greeks.* He is also a well-known translator.

AGATHE THORNTON is the author of *People and Themes in Homer's* Odyssey.

C. M. BOWRA was Professor of Poetry at Oxford. His books include *The Greek Experience, Tradition and Design in the* Iliad, *Ancient Greek Literature,* and *Periclean Athens.*

NORMAN AUSTIN is Professor of Classics at the University of Massachusetts, Amherst.

HELENE P. FOLEY is Professor of Greek and Latin at Columbia University. Her books include *Reflections of Women in Antiquity* and *Ritual Irony: Poetry and Sacrifice in Euripides.*

JENNY STRAUSS CLAY is Professor of Classics at the University of Virginia.

CHARLES SEGAL is Professor of Classics at Brown University. His books include *Landscape in Ovid's* Metamorphoses, *Tragedy and Civilization, Poetry and Myth in Ancient Pastoral,* and *Dionysiac Poetics and Euripides'* Bacchae, in addition to many articles.

153

Bibliography

Abrahamson, Ernest. *The Adventure of Odysseus*. St. Louis: Washington University Press, 1960.

Adkins, A. W. H. "Honor and Punishment in the Homeric Poems." *Bulletin of the Institute of Classical Studies* 7 (1960): 23–32.

Amory, Anne. "The Gates of Horn and Ivory." *Yale Classical Studies* 20 (1966): 3–57.

Austin, Norman. *Archery at the Dark of the Moon*. Berkeley: University of California Press, 1975.

Belmont, David E. "Twentieth-Century Odysseus." *Classical Journal* 62 (1966): 49–56.

Bertman, S. "The Telemachy and Structural Symmetry." *Transactions of the American Philological Association* 97 (1966): 15–27.

Beye, Charles R. The Iliad, The Odyssey *and The Epic Tradition*. Garden City, N.Y.: Doubleday, 1966.

Bowra, C. M. *Homer*. London: Duckworth, 1972.

Bradford, Ernie. *Ulysses Found*. London: Hodder & Stoughton, 1963.

Bradley, Edward M. "The Hubris of Odysseus." *Soundings* 51 (1968): 33–44.

———. "The Greatness of His Nature." *Ramus* 5 (1976): 137–48.

Brown, C. S. "Odysseus and Polyphemus: The Name and the Curse." *Comparative Literature* 18 (1966): 193–202.

Burrows, R. Z. "Deception as a Comic Device in the *Odyssey*." *Classical World* 59 (1965): 33–36.

Camps, W. A. *An Introduction to Homer*. Oxford: Clarendon, 1980.

Clarke, H. W. "Telemachus and the Telemachia." *American Journal of Philology* 84 (1963): 129–45.

Clay, Jenny Strauss. *The Wrath of Athena*. Princeton: Princeton University Press, 1983.

Damon, Philip. "Dilation and Displacement in the *Odyssey*." *Pacific Coast Philology* 5 (1970): 19–23.

de Almeida, Hermione. *Byron and Joyce through Homer*. London: Macmillan, 1981.

Dietrich, B. C. "The Spinning of Fate in Homer." *Phoenix* 16 (1962): 86–101.

———. *Death, Fate and the Gods*. London: Athlone, 1965.

Dimock, George. "Crime and Punishment in the *Odyssey*." *Yale Review* 60 (1971): 199–214.

Dyck, A. R. "The Witch's Bed but Not Her Breakfast." *Rheinisches Museum für Philologie* 124 (1982): 196–298.

Else, G. E. *Homer and the Homeric Problem*. Cincinnati: University of Cincinnati Press, 1965.

Fantazzi, Charles. "Courtly Odysseus." *International Homeric Symposium* 2 (1969): 33–37.

Fenik, Bernard. *Studies in the Odyssey*. Hermes, vol. 30. Wiesbaden: Franz Steiner, 1974.

———, ed. *Homer: Tradition and Invention*. Leiden: E. J. Brill, 1978.

Finley, John H., Jr. *Homer's Odyssey*. Cambridge: Harvard University Press, 1978.

Flaumenhaft, Mera J. "The Undercover Hero." *Interpretation* 10, 1 (1982): 9–41.

Frame, Douglas. *The Myth of Return in Early Greek Epic*. New Haven: Yale University Press, 1978.

Friedrich, R. "On the Compositional Use of Similes in the *Odyssey*." *American Journal of Philology* 102 (1981): 120–37.

Griffin, Jasper. *Homer on Life and Death*. Oxford: Clarendon, 1980.

Gross, Nicholas P. "Nausicaa: A Feminine Threat." *Classical World* 69 (1976): 311–17.

Hansen, William F. *The Conference Sequence*. Berkeley and Los Angeles: University of California Press, 1972.

———. "Odysseus' Last Journey." *Quaderni Urbinati di Cultura Classica* 24 (1977): 27–48.

Harrison, E. L. "Notes on Homeric Psychology." *Phoenix* 14 (1960): 63–80.

Havelock, Eric A. *Preface to Plato*. Cambridge: Harvard University Press, 1963.

Heatherington, M. E. "Chaos, Order, and Cunning in the *Odyssey*." *Studies in Philology* 83 (1976): 225–39.

Hogan, J. C. "The Temptation of Odysseus." *Transactions of the American Philological Association* 106 (1976): 187–210.

Holtsmark, E. B. "Spiritual Rebirth of the Hero: *Odyssey* V." *Classical Journal* 61 (1966): 206–10.

Kearns, Emily. "The Return of Odysseus." *The Classical Quarterly* 76 (1982): 2–8.

Kelly, M. N. "Pictorial Formalism in the *Odyssey*?" *La Parola del Passato* 20 (1965): 48–50.

Kirk, G. S. "Homer and Modern Oral Poetry: Some Confusions." *Classical Quarterly* 54 (1960): 271–81.

———. *The Songs of Homer*. Cambridge: Cambridge University Press, 1962.

———, ed. *The Language and Background of Homer*. Cambridge: W. Heffer, 1964.

Kitto, H. D. F. *Poiesis*. Berkeley: University of California Press, 1966.

Lidov, Joel B. "The Anger of Poseidon." *Arethusa* 10 (1977): 227–36.

Lloyd-Jones, Hugh. *The Justice of Zeus*. Berkeley and Los Angeles: University of California Press, 1971.

Lord, A. B. *The Singer of Tales*. Harvard Studies in Comparative Literature, vol. 24. Cambridge: Harvard University Press, 1960.

Nagler, Michael N. *Spontaneity and Tradition*. Berkeley and Los Angeles: University of California Press, 1974.

Nelson, Conny, ed. *Homer's Odyssey: A Critical Handbook*. Belmont, Calif.: Wadsworth, 1969.

Niles, John D. "Patterning in the Wanderings of the *Odyssey.*" *Ramus* 6 (1978): 46–60.

Page, Denys. *Folktales in Homer's* Odyssey. Cambridge: Harvard University Press, 1973.

Plass, P. "Menelaus and Proteus." *Classical Journal* 65 (1969): 104–8.

Pocock, L. G. *Odyssean Essays.* Oxford: Basil Blackwell, 1965.

Podlecki, A. J. "Guest-Gifts and Nobodies in *Odyssey* 9." *Phoenix* 15 (1961): 125–33.

Powell, Barry B. *Composition by Theme in the* Odyssey. Meisenheim am Glan: Verlag Anton Hain, 1977.

Pucci, Pietro. "The Song of the Sirens." *Arethusa* 12 (1979): 121–32.

Rexroth, Kenneth. "Homer's *Odyssey.*" Classics Revisited. New York: New Directions, 1965.

Rose, G. P. "The Unfriendly Phaeacians." *Transactions of the American Philological Association* 100 (1969): 387–406.

Russo, Joseph. "Interview and Aftermath: Dream, Fantasy, and Intuition in *Odyssey* 19 and 20." *American Journal of Philology* 103 (1982): 4–18.

Segal, Charles P. "The Phaeacians and the Symbolism of Odysseus' Return." *Arion* 4 (1964): 17–64.

———. "Transitions and Ritual in Odysseus' Return." *La Parola del Passato* 22 (1967): 321–42.

Stanford, W. B. "The Ending of the *Odyssey*: An Ethical Approach." *Hermathema* 100 (1965): 5–20.

Stewart, Douglas. *The Disguised Guest.* Lewisburg, Pa.: Bucknell University Press, 1975.

Taylor, Charles H. *Essays on the* Odyssey. Bloomington: Indiana University Press, 1963.

Taylor, Charles T. "The Obstacles to Odysseus' Return: Identity and Consciousness in *The Odyssey.*" *Yale Review* 51 (1961): 569–80.

Thornton, Agathe. *People and Themes in Homer's* Odyssey. London: Methuen, 1970.

Vivante, Paolo. "Homer and the Aesthetic Movement." *Arion* 4 (1965): 415–38.

———. "On the Representation of Nature and Reality in Homer." *Arion* 5 (1966): 149–90.

———. *The Homeric Imagination.* Bloomington: Indiana University Press, 1970.

———. "Rose-Fingered Dawn and the Idea of Time." *Ramus* 8 (1980): 125–36.

———. *Homer.* New Haven: Yale University Press, 1985.

Walcott, P. "Odysseus and the Art of Lying." *Ancient Society* 8 (1977): 1–19.

Acknowledgments

"The *Odyssey:* The Exclusion of Surprise" (originally entitled "*The Odyssey*") by H. D. F. Kitto from *Poiesis: Structure and Thought* by H. D. F. Kitto, © 1966 by the Regents of the University of California. Reprinted by permission of the University of California Press.

"The Homecomings of the Achaeans" by Agathe Thornton from *People and Themes in Homer's* Odyssey by Agathe Thornton, © 1970 by Agathe Thornton. Reprinted by permission of the author, Methuen & Co., and the University of Otago Press, Dunedin, New Zealand.

"The *Odyssey:* Its Shape and Character" by C. M. Bowra from *Homer* by C. M. Bowra, © 1972 by the Estate of C. M. Bowra. Reprinted by permission of Gerald Duckworth and Co. Ltd.

"The Power of the Word" (originally entitled "From Cities to Mind") by Norman Austin from *Archery at the Dark of the Moon* by Norman Austin, © 1975 by the Regents of the University of California. Reprinted by permission of the University of California Press.

" 'Reverse Similes' and Sex Roles in the *Odyssey*" by Helene P. Foley from *Arethusa* 11, nos. 1–2 (Spring/Fall 1978), © 1978 by the Department of Classics, State University of New York at Buffalo. Reprinted by permission.

"Odysseus: Name and Helmet" (originally entitled "Odysseus") by Jenny Strauss Clay from *The Wrath of Athena* by Jenny Strauss Clay, © 1983 by Princeton University Press. Reprinted by permission of Princeton University Press.

"Kleos and Its Ironies in the *Odyssey*" by Charles Segal from *L'Antiquité Classique* 52 (1983), © 1983 by the University of Brussels. Reprinted by permission.

Index

Achaeans, 35, 36, 37, 43, 44–47, 110

Achilles: Agamemnon and, 39, 40–41, 42, 53, 115; appearance of ghost of, 39, 40–42, 53; ash spear of, 119; contest for arms of, 113, 115; death and funeral of, 40, 41, 43; and defying of gods, 111–12; double meaning of name of, 110; Hector and, 111–12; as hero of *Iliad*, 1–2, 10, 110, 111; horse of, 62; kleos of, 127, 129–30, 131; Odysseus and, 1, 2, 40, 41–42, 65, 66; Patroclus and, 101, 110; Suitors contrasted with, 9, 53; as symbol of might, 41, 42; wrath of, 1, 2, 9, 66, 111–12

Aegisthus, 14, 35–36, 37, 44, 46, 47, 65

Aegyptius, 21, 22

Aeneas (*Iliad*), 1, 2, 62, 111

Aeolus, 62, 95

Aeschylus, 18; *Agamemnon*, 15, 21, 104; *Choephori*, 17; *Eumenides*, 19, 37, 95; *Supplices*, 19

Agamemnon, 52, 140; Achilles and, 39, 40–41, 42, 53, 115; Amphimedon and, 41; appearance of ghost of, 37, 52; betrayal and murder of, 35–36, 37, 40, 44, 46, 47, 52, 135; homecoming of, 10, 35–36, 42–43, 46; as illustrating failure of traditional kleos, 135, 137; Menelaus and, 43, 118; Odysseus and, 36, 37, 40, 42, 135–36, 148; on Penelope, 37, 42, 53, 135; scepter of,

118–19, 120; on spy mission, 117, 118

Agamemnon (Aeschylus), 15, 21, 104

Aias, 52, 53

Aidos (shame), 134–35, 136

Ajax, 2, 10, 39, 46, 115–16

Alcinous, 65, 80–81, 82–83, 90, 98–99; Odysseus and, 72–73, 79, 81–82, 83–85, 128, 138, 148

Amphidamas, 120, 121, 122

Amphimedon, 40, 41, 60, 135, 148

Amphinomus, 27, 28, 65

Amyntor, 121, 122

Antheus (Agathon), 15

Antigone (Sophocles), 15

Antilochus, 39, 53

Antinous, 18, 20, 21, 22, 23, 27; characterization of, 36, 64–65

Aphrodite, 62, 108, 111; and song of Demodocus, 65, 91

Apollo, 28–29, 44, 111, 122. *See also* Helios

Ares, 65, 91, 108

Arete, 72, 75, 79, 80, 81, 84, 85; harmonious marriage of, 82–83, 98–99

Argus, 24, 58, 59

Aristarchus, 61

Aristophanes, 61, 88

Aristotle, 5, 8, 11, 15, 30; on Homer, 31, 32, 33

Arnaeus. *See* Irus

As You Like It (Shakespeare), 97

Athena, 16, 38, 66, 122; anger of, 43, 110, 112; as helping Odysseus, 8, 14, 15, 17, 18, 28, 29, 37, 38, 39, 58, 62, 148; as helping

161

and, 12, 14, 17, 20, 21–22, 23, 36,
54; theme called Comedy of Manners, 7, 8, 9, 18, 50
Supplices (Aeschylus), 19

Teiresias. *See* Tiresias
Telemachus: Athena and, 9, 12, 14, 17,
20, 21, 29, 37, 38, 66, 77; as dup-
licating experiences of Odysseus,
70–74, 78; Helen and, 72, 75–76;
increase in mental powers of, 77–
78; and journey to Sparta, 8–9, 12,
20, 51, 54, 72, 73, 74–77; maturing of, 19, 20–21, 54, 64, 70–71,
74, 76–78, 91; Menelaus and, 39–
40, 45, 46, 51, 71, 72, 73, 74, 75,
76–77; Nestor and, 37, 41, 71, 73,
74, 142; Odysseus and, 58, 88, 95–
96, 106, 149; and parallels with
Orestes, 36, 37; Penelope and, 20,
21, 28–29, 89–90, 91, 99, 144; and
prayer to Zeus and Apollo, 28–29;
Suitors and, 12, 14, 17, 20, 21–22,
23, 28, 36, 54; Theoclymenus and,
60; and voyage to Pylos, 12, 20,
51, 64, 73–74; Zeus and, 14, 22,
23, 77

Télémaque et la structure de l'Odyssée
(Delabecque), 9
Tennyson, Alfred, Lord, 2, 3
Theoclymenus, 38, 60–61, 72, 77
Thersites, 52, 64
Tiresias, 58, 71
Trojan War, 10, 11, 40, 42, 111; shift of
attitude toward, 51; tales of, 110,
113, 117
Troy, 11, 35, 40, 51, 54, 66, 75–76

Ulysses. *See* Odysseus
Ulysses 4 (Alcidamas), 124

Vidal-Naquet, P., 93
Virgil, 2

Wooden Horse, 10, 42, 72, 76; Odysseus as mastermind of, 113
Works and Days (Hesiod), 95

Zeus: on Aegisthus, 35, 36, 37; and Argives, 43, 44; Deception of, 65;
Odysseus and, 14–15, 112; "programmatic" speech of, 36; and relations with mortal women, 95;
social achievements of, 95; Telemachus and, 14, 23, 28–29, 77